To GGAH

Special thanks to Margaret Crawford, Elizabeth Koch, Sylvie Leprohon and Steve Hodgson for their invaluable suggestions during the creation of this book.

Please go forth and Supercharge Your Flute Technique but do not supercharge your photocopier. This book is protected under Australian copyright law (Copyright Act 1968) and any reproduction either mechanical or electronic is illegal. This book is not covered by any performing rights association agreements and making copies breaches the rights of the author over any intellectual property contained within. On a lighter note it is easy to obtain further copies of this book at peterbartelsflute.com or ask your favourite music retailer or website to stock this volume. Use the ISBN/barcode on the back cover to identify this book.

©Peter Bartels 2017 All Rights Reserved
ISBN 978-0-648-05720-8
Melbourne, Victoria, Australia
Cover design: Arthur Angelo

Introduction

In my usual teaching week I have the joy of working with the youngest of beginners through to advanced tertiary students. Over the years I have noticed there are ample resources for young students and plenty of books for advanced players but not much material to bridge the gap between the two. This book is borne from the need to traverse that gap. It contains a plethora of exercises I have created and used over many years, in order for you to Supercharge Your Flute Technique.

The book is divided into seven chapters focusing on different aspects of playing. The first chapter is for the player who is new to focused technical work while the final chapter provides some ideas for the more advanced player to structure their technical practice. In between you'll discover plenty of exercises on scales, arpeggios, broken chords, chromatics, thirds and even a chapter on practising difficult passages.

At first glance some of the exercises may appear straightforward but don't be deceived by this apparent simplicity as they should only be treated as a template for further study. Learn to play them in all major and minor keys adjusting the range, tempi and articulation for your level of playing. You can make the exercises as easy or as challenging as you like.

It is imperative to use a metronome, adjusting the given tempi as required. Articulation patterns are suggestions and a wide variety of patterns should be employed.

By mixing the keys, range, tempi and articulation patterns you can alter any of the exercises to make them your own. Use the exercises as a springboard to make your technical practice varied and interesting. It is worth the effort as the ability to play quickly, evenly and effortlessly enables the player to come out from behind the notes and present their musical message with increased conviction and engagement.

There is no need to work through the book in order. Find the exercises that you like and master them first. Eventually you should aim to learn all the exercises in all keys, at fast tempi, over the entire range!

So good luck and have fun supercharging your flute technique!

Peter Bartels

Table Of Contents

Starting out — 6
Finger Buster in F major — 7
Finger Buster in G major — 7
Finger Buster in C major — 7
Finger Buster in D harmonic minor — 8
Finger Buster in E harmonic minor — 8
Finger Buster in A harmonic minor — 8
Finger Buster in D melodic minor — 9
Finger Buster in E melodic minor — 9
Finger Buster in A melodic minor — 9
Half scales major keys — 10
Half scales minor keys — 12
Major half scales with their triad — 14
Minor half scales with their triad — 16
Sequential half scales plus triads — 18
One octave major scales and arpeggios — 20
One octave harmonic minor scales and arpeggios — 22
One octave melodic minor scales and arpeggios — 24
Semibreves to demisemiquavers — 26

Scales — 29
Modal scales with a minim at the top — 30
Continuous modal scales — 31
Loopy scale challenge — 32
The original scale challenge — 33
Sequential scale challenge — 35
Triplet-gigue scale challenge — 35
Block scales — 36
Intensive five note scale blitz — 37
Six-eight fine finger movement — 38
Nine-eight fine finger movement — 42
Fibonacci scale — 47
Simplified fibonacci scale — 48
Building a scale from the top — 50
Whole tone scales — 52

Arpeggios and broken chords — 53
Building an arpeggio — 54
Repeating intervals — 56
Arpeggio in three-eight — 56
Arpeggios by threes — 57
Breaking up broken chords — 59
Semiquaver broken chords — 60
Continuously expanding arpeggio — 61

Diminished arpeggios and broken chords	62
Diminished 7th arpeggios	63
Dominant 7th arpeggios and broken chords	65

Chromatics — 68

Chromatic corners	69
Climbing chromatics	70
Repeated semiquaver blocks	71
Pausing on the beat	73
Pausing at the octave	73
Pillar notes	74
The four augmented triads	75
Octave leaps	76
Tied up nine-eight chromatic	78
Six-eight chromatic by step	80

Scales in thirds — 82

Rising and descending thirds	83
Thirds in three four	84
Manageable blocks by step	85
Manageable blocks ascending and descending	86
Looping around	87
Building up your scales in thirds	88
Scales in thirds over the entire range	89

Working on challenging passages — 91

Using rhythms on a run	92
Pausing on each note	93
Rhythmic alterations in compound time	95
Pausing on each note in compound time	96
The backwards game	98
The forwards game	100
Forward fibonacci run	102
Backward fibonacci run	104

Organising your practice — 106

Cycle of fifths	107
Brushing your teeth	108
Key of the week	109
Charts	111
Everything from a single pitch	112

Starting out

Finger Busters

In order to develop your flute technique and get really flashy fingers you will need to do more than just play your scales ascending and descending. You probably already know some scales so try these Finger Buster patterns to make your scales more challenging and more amazing.

The harmonic minor Finger Busters sound a bit clunky around the 7th note but it is important that you learn this part of the scale thoroughly. Following on from the three harmonic minor Finger Busters are the melodic minor versions which sound a lot smoother and are more pleasing to the ear.

Finger Buster in D harmonic minor

Finger Buster in E harmonic minor

Finger Buster in A harmonic minor

Finger Buster in D melodic minor

Finger Buster in E melodic minor

Finger Buster in A melodic minor

Now try all the Finger Busters in as many different keys as you can.

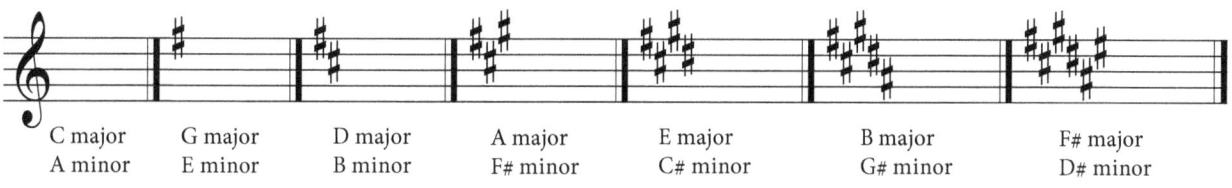

©Peter Bartels 2017
peterbartelsflute.com

Half scales major keys

A good place to start broadening your knowledge of scales is with half scales. As the name suggests, a half scale limits the range to only half an octave which is very manageable. Begin with G major and F major as they have just one sharp and flat each and then gradually add in more keys until you can play all the keys. There are also four articulation patterns that you can try out on the half scales if you are feeling daring.

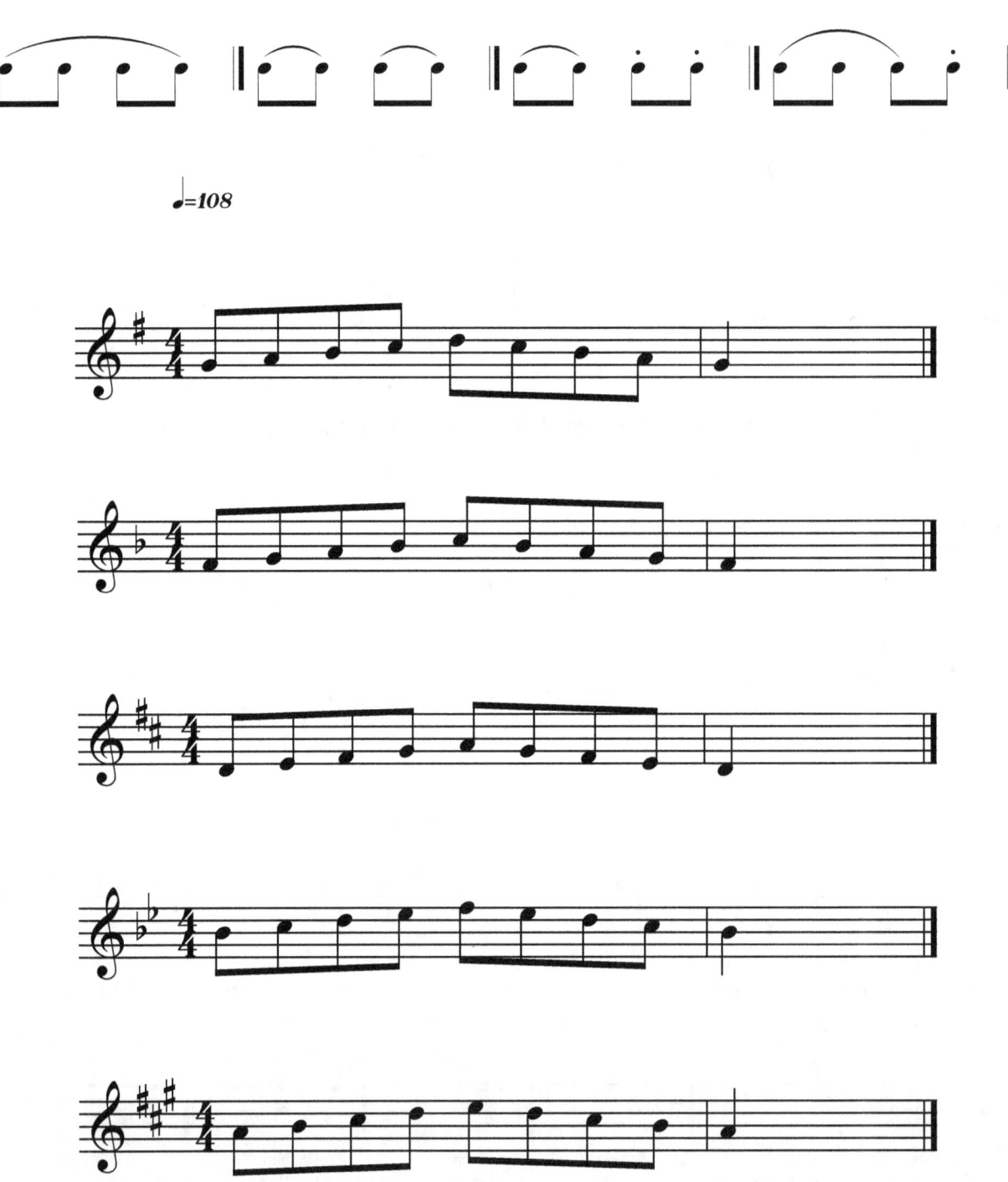

Starting out 11

Half scales minor keys

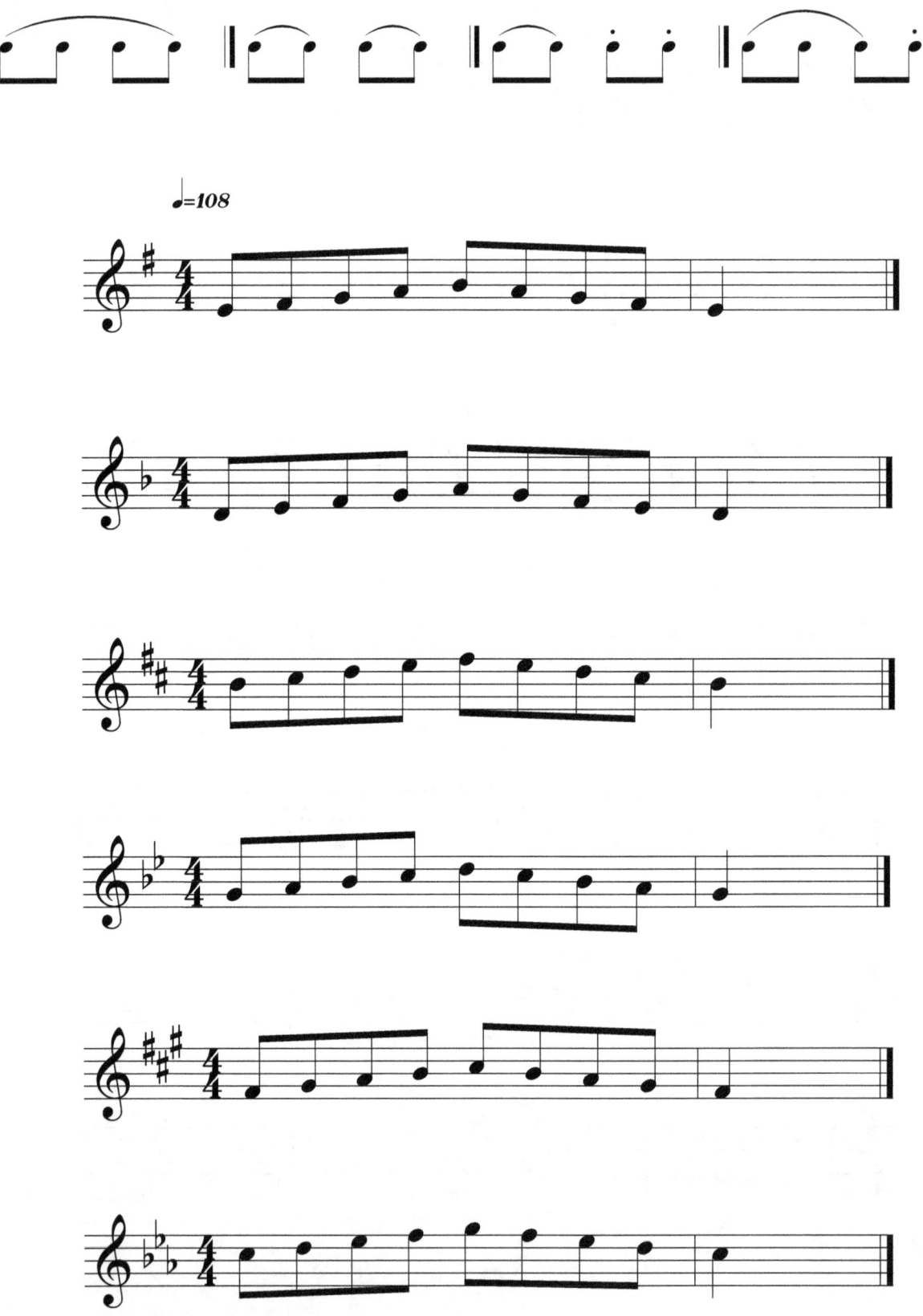

Major half scales with their triad

By now you should know your half scales. Here they are again but the triad has been added onto the end. Don't forget to challenge yourself by trying the different articulation patterns as well.

Starting out 15

Minor half scales with their triad

In addition to playing the half scales with their triad in all the major keys, you can learn your half scales with their triads in the minor keys as well.

Sequential half scales plus triads

This tricky exercise is based on the half scales with their triads but stays within the one key. The same pattern of notes is used but moves by step each bar so that it commences on each note of the scale.

Here is a twisty variation on the previous exercise which puts the ascending pattern and the descending pattern next to each other.

©Peter Bartels 2017
peterbartelsflute.com

Now work your way through the sequential half scales plus triads in as many keys as you can. Try all the major and minor keys.

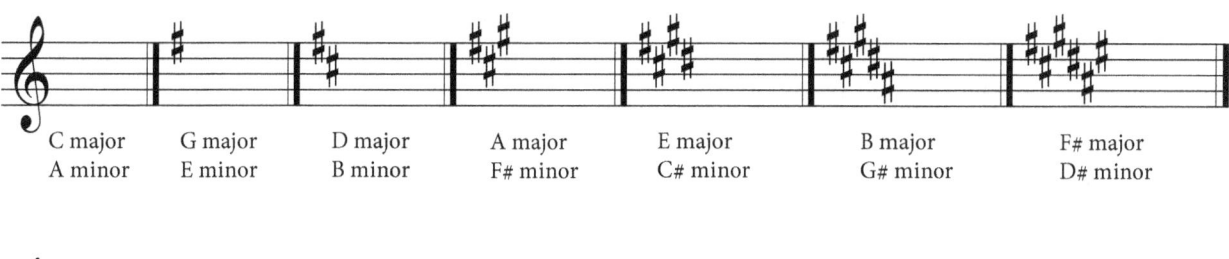

C major   G major   D major   A major   E major   B major   F# major
A minor   E minor   B minor   F# minor   C# minor   G# minor   D# minor

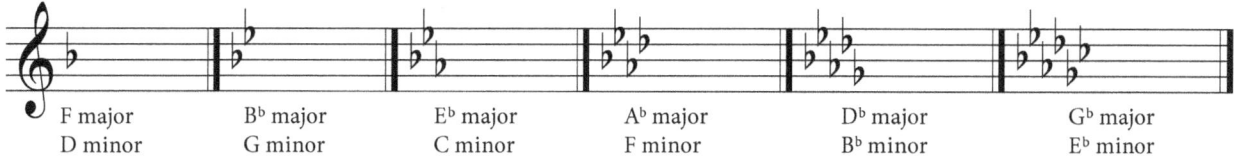

F major   B♭ major   E♭ major   A♭ major   D♭ major   G♭ major
D minor   G minor   C minor   F minor   B♭ minor   E♭ minor

One octave major scales and arpeggios

Up until this point, the exercises have mainly focussed on half scales. Now go wild and try putting it all together with the following six pages of one octave scales and arpeggios in all the major, harmonic and melodic minor keys using the different articulation patterns as well. These one octave scales wind their way around the cycle of fifths and eventually end up back where they started.

One octave harmonic minor scales and arpeggios

One octave melodic minor scales and arpeggios

Semibreves to demisemiquavers

Here is a method of working that can help you to learn any scale that you are not sure of. This example uses E major.

   1. First of all make sure you can say all the notes of the scale without your flute in your hands.

   2. Now with your flute in your hands say the notes of the scale and then put your fingers on for that note. Be sure you put your fingers on AFTER you have said the note and not before. Avoid reading the notes off your fingers but rather think the note first and then place your fingers on the keys.

   3. Play the exercise below using your metronome. It consolidates the notes slowly and then gradually increases the tempo. With the final demisemiquaver line play it as quickly as you can ensuring that you hear every single note of the scale.

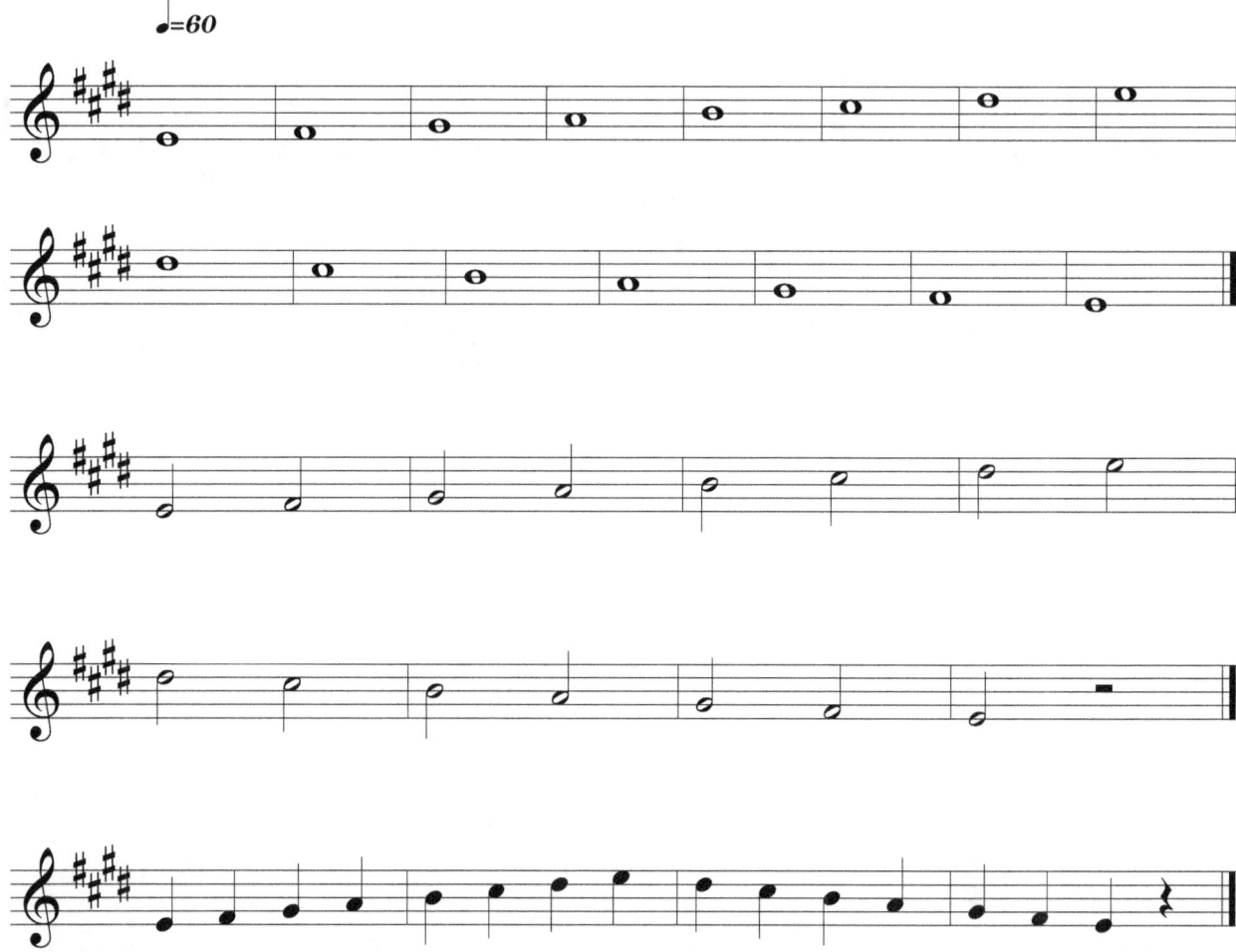

Scales

Modal scales with a minim at the top

This chapter contains a variety of different ways that you can practice your scales. The exercises are given as a template in G major but of course you should learn to play them in all major and minor keys. The range of the exercises can be adjusted as you wish. If your flute has a low B then maybe you want to go down to low B. If you want to play up to top B then do that or extend right up to top D. It's up to you. Being rhythmically stable and playing evenly is an important hallmark of a good technique so be sure to use your metronome frequently. This first exercise uses the same pattern sequentially from each note of the scale so it plays through all the modes; ionian, dorian, phrygian lydian, mixolydian, aeolian and locrian.

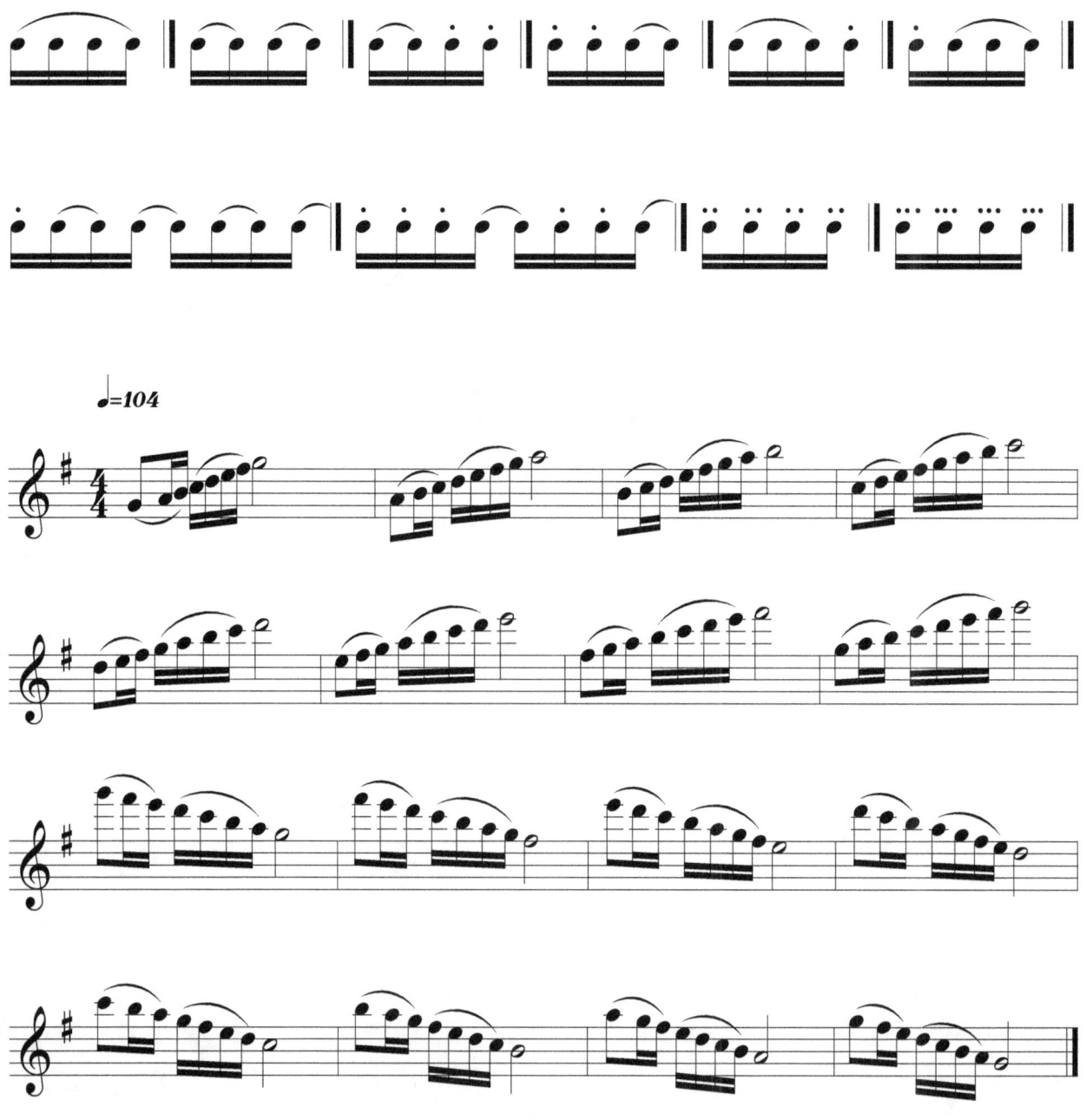

Continuous modal scales

The next exercise is similar to the previous one but it doesn't have the minim at the top so it is going to test out your concentration. Try this exercise and the previous version over a two octave range or even over the entire range.

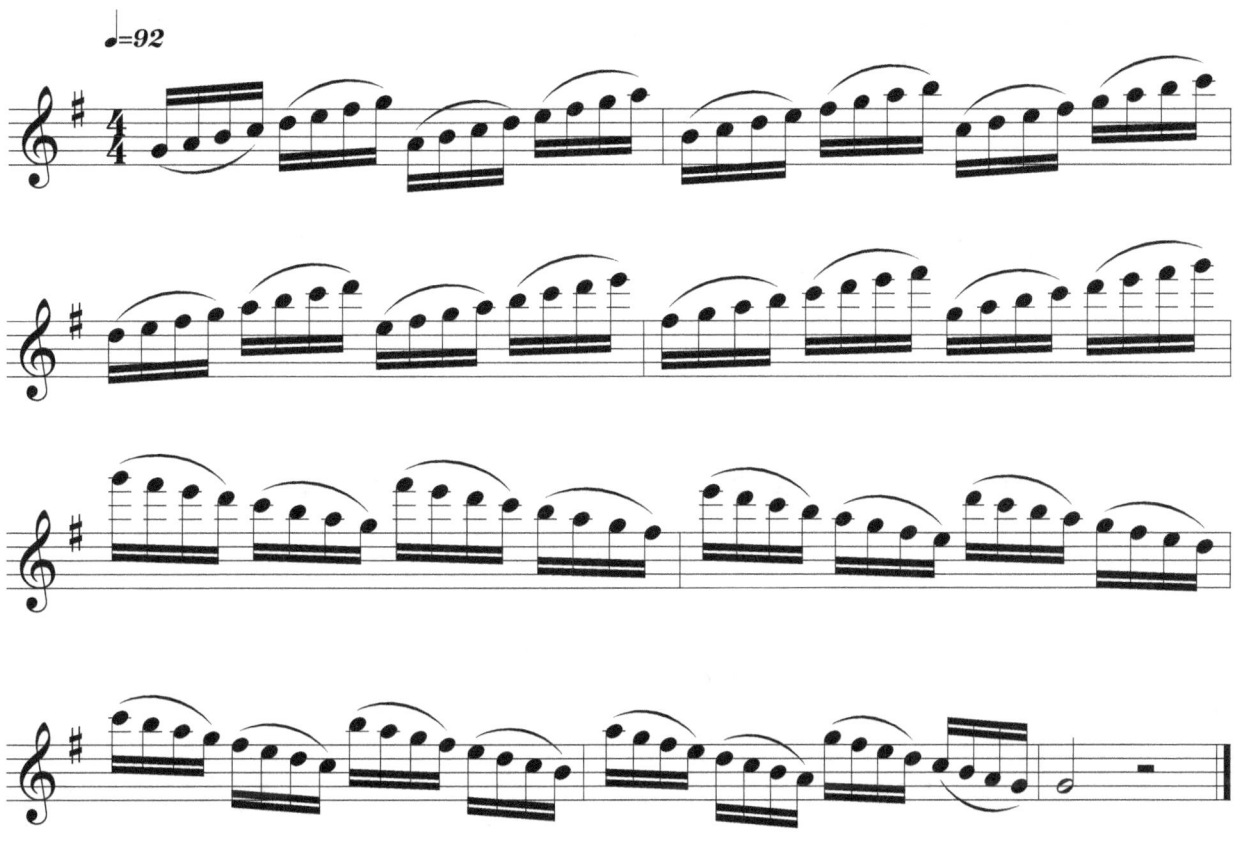

Play both the modal scales exercises in all key areas.

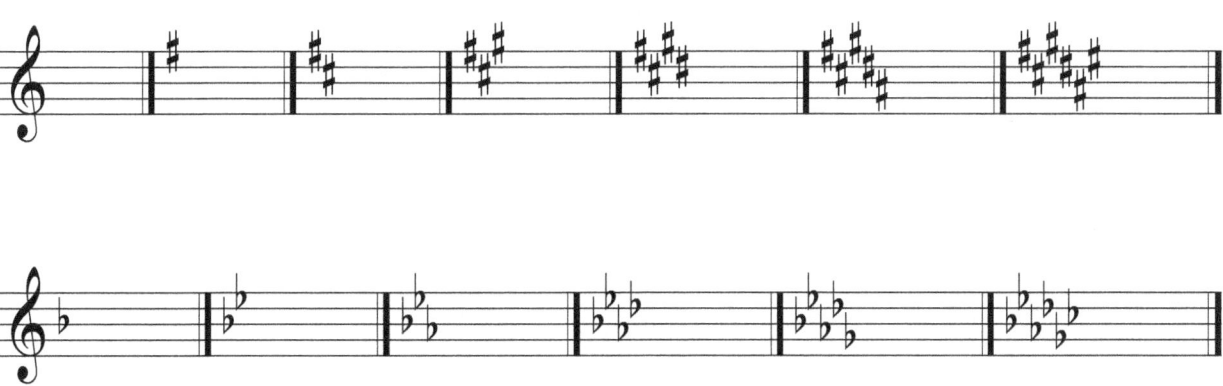

Scale challenges

The following four exercises are what I call scale challenges. There is the Loopy Scale Challenge, the Original Scale Challenge, the Sequential Scale Challenge and the Triplet-Gigue Scale Challenge. You may initially like to play these four exercises with a range of just one octave or perhaps even work on the second octave separately. Then of course transpose the four scale challenges into every major and minor key. Aim to keep your fingers curved, relaxed and placed precisely on the keys. Your metronome should be getting a good work out and your tongue as well.

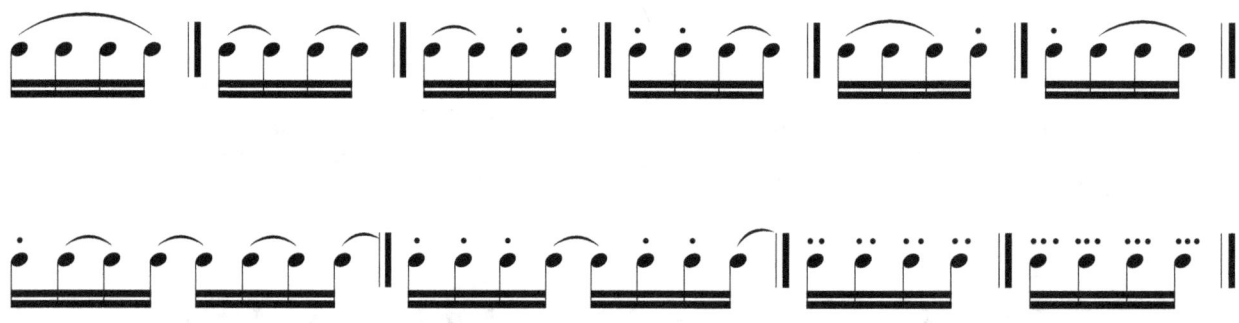

Loopy scale challenge

The original scale challenge

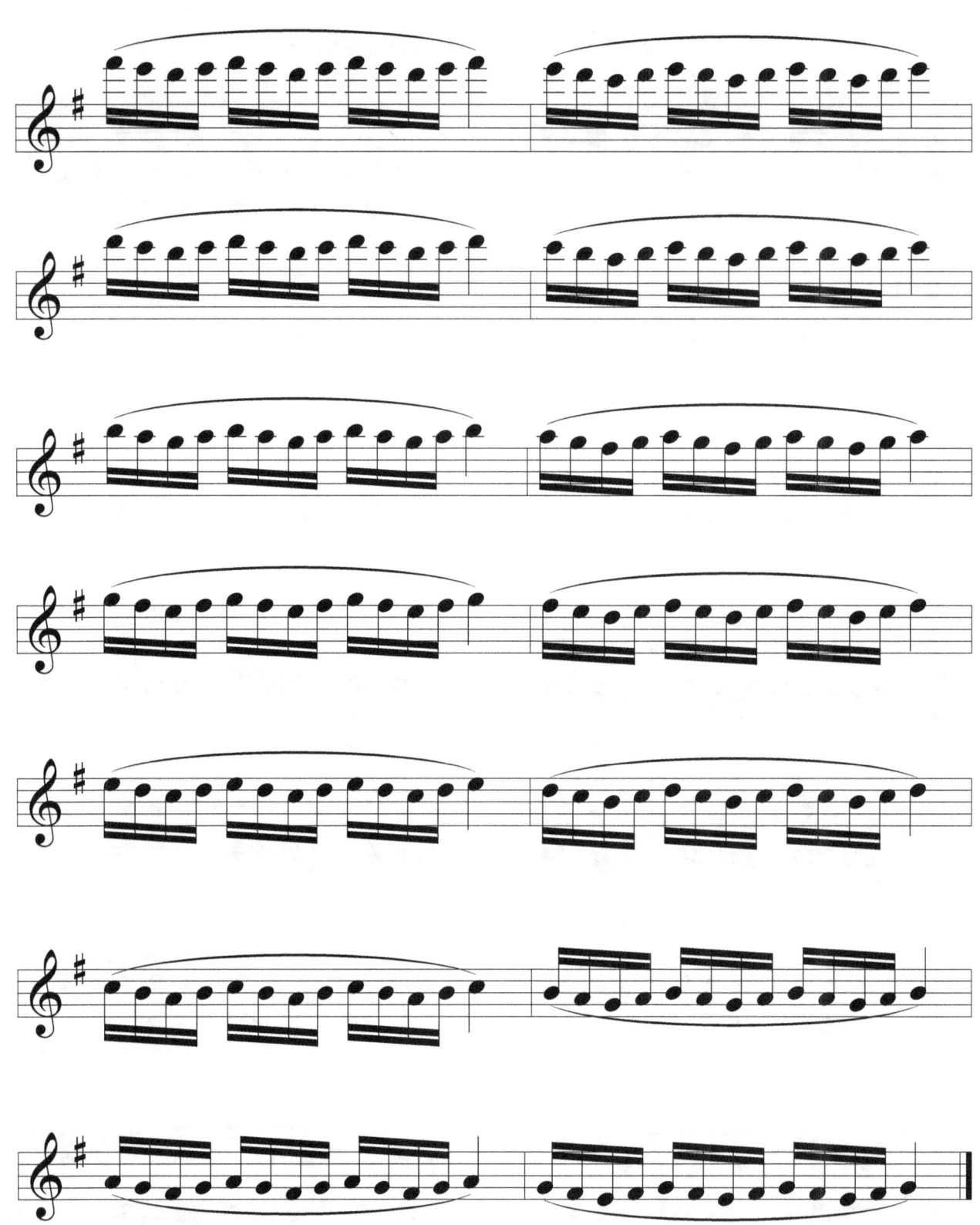

Sequential scale challenge

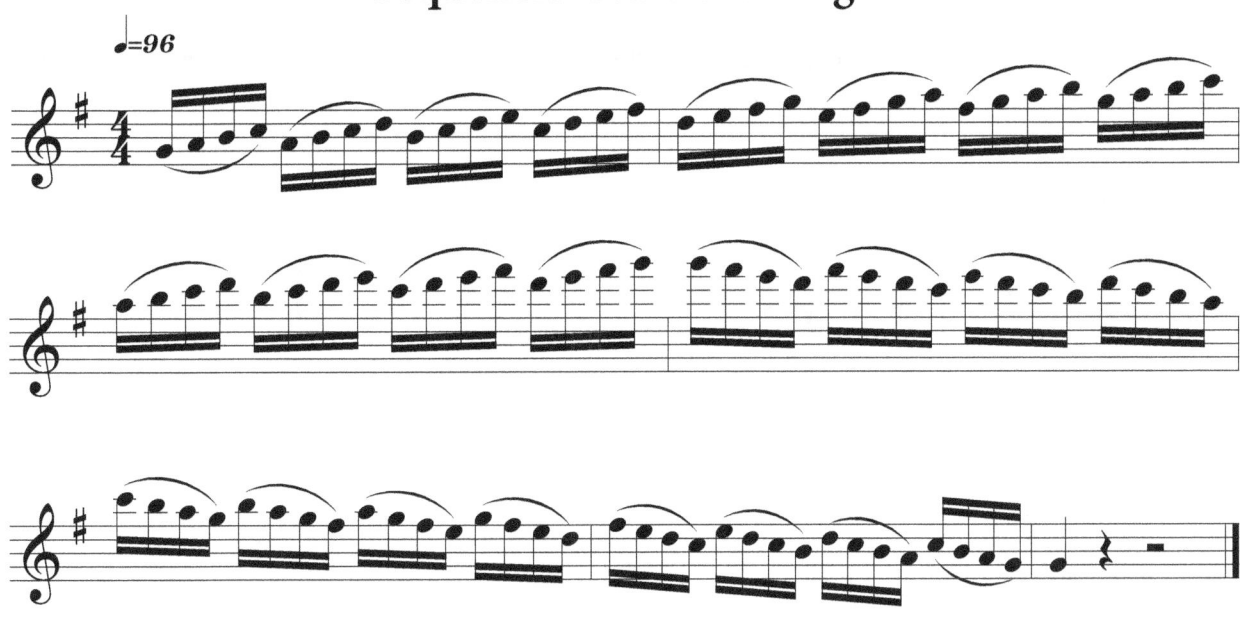

Triplet-gigue scale challenge

©Peter Bartels 2017
peterbartelsflute.com

Block scales

The following exercise builds up the scales in blocks of semiquavers. Play the repeats as many times as you need to in order to get each group fast and even.

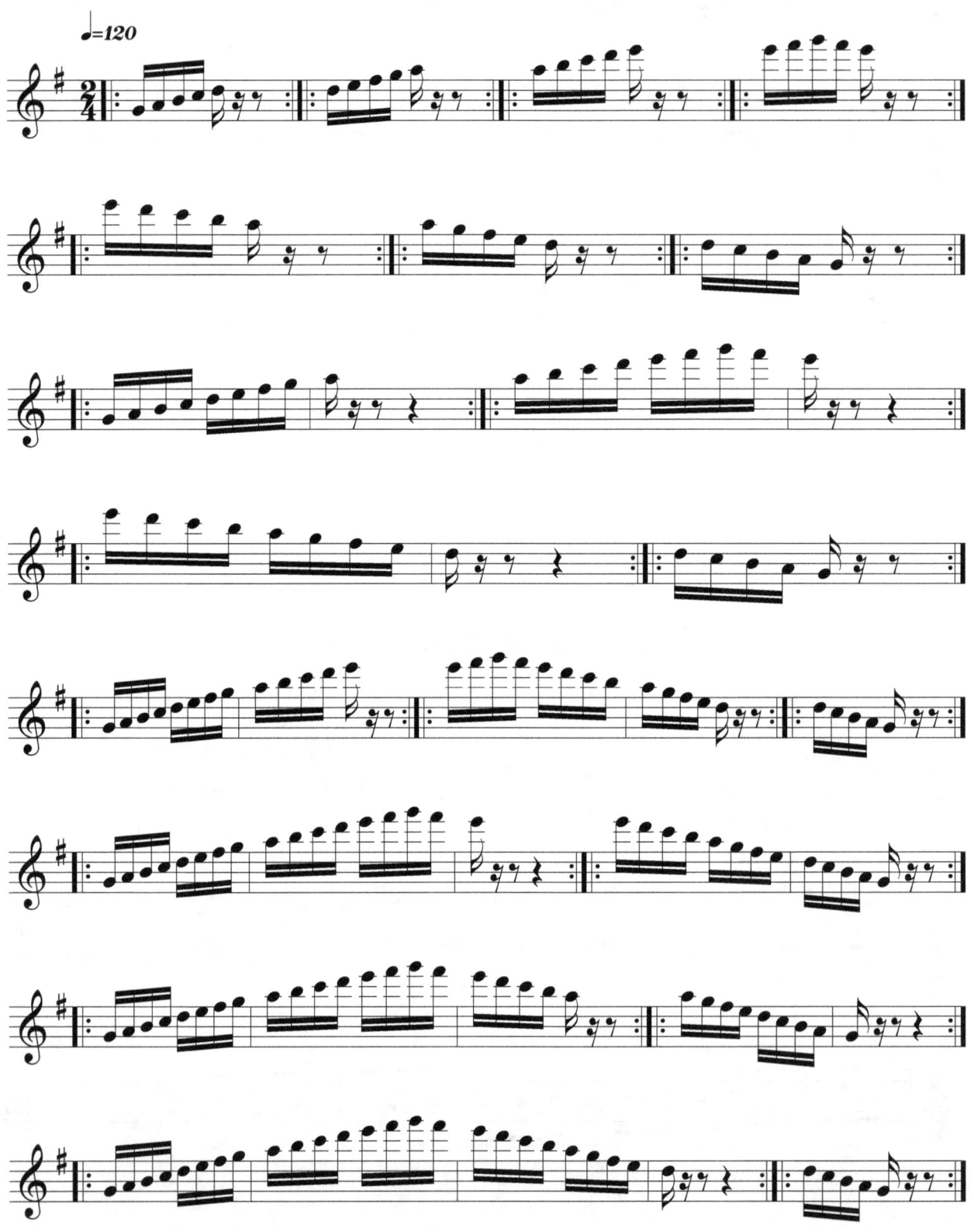

Intensive five note scale blitz

This exercise is based on the well known five note exercise but takes it up a level. The first line below uses the first five notes of the G major scale. The second line uses the same five notes but starts on the second note of the group. Follow this with the third note of the group and finally the last note in the group. Repeat each line as many times as you need to make it fluent. Once you have done this move onto the second note of the G major scale and follow the same pattern. So your five notes will now be A B C D E. Then commence on B, C and so on until you have made your way right through the scale. Of course, all keys both major and minor. You could also change the articulation pattern.

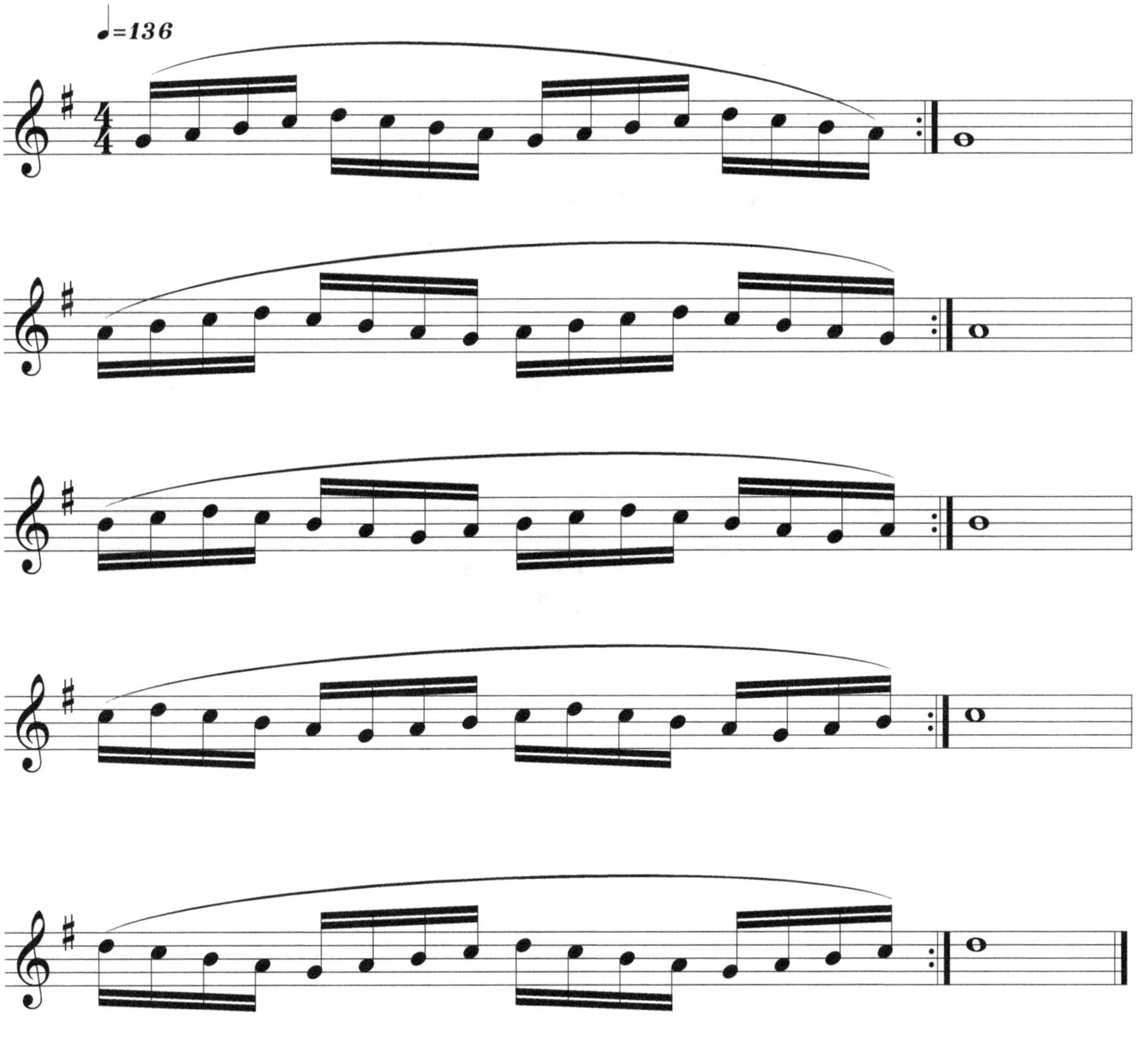

Six-eight fine finger movement

The following exercise is quite intense as it works on every note in the scale. Remember to strive for relaxed hands and minimal finger movement. Rather than starting this exercise on the tonic you could extend the range by commencing on low C and continue up as high as you want before returning to low C to finish. Play this exercise in every major and minor key.

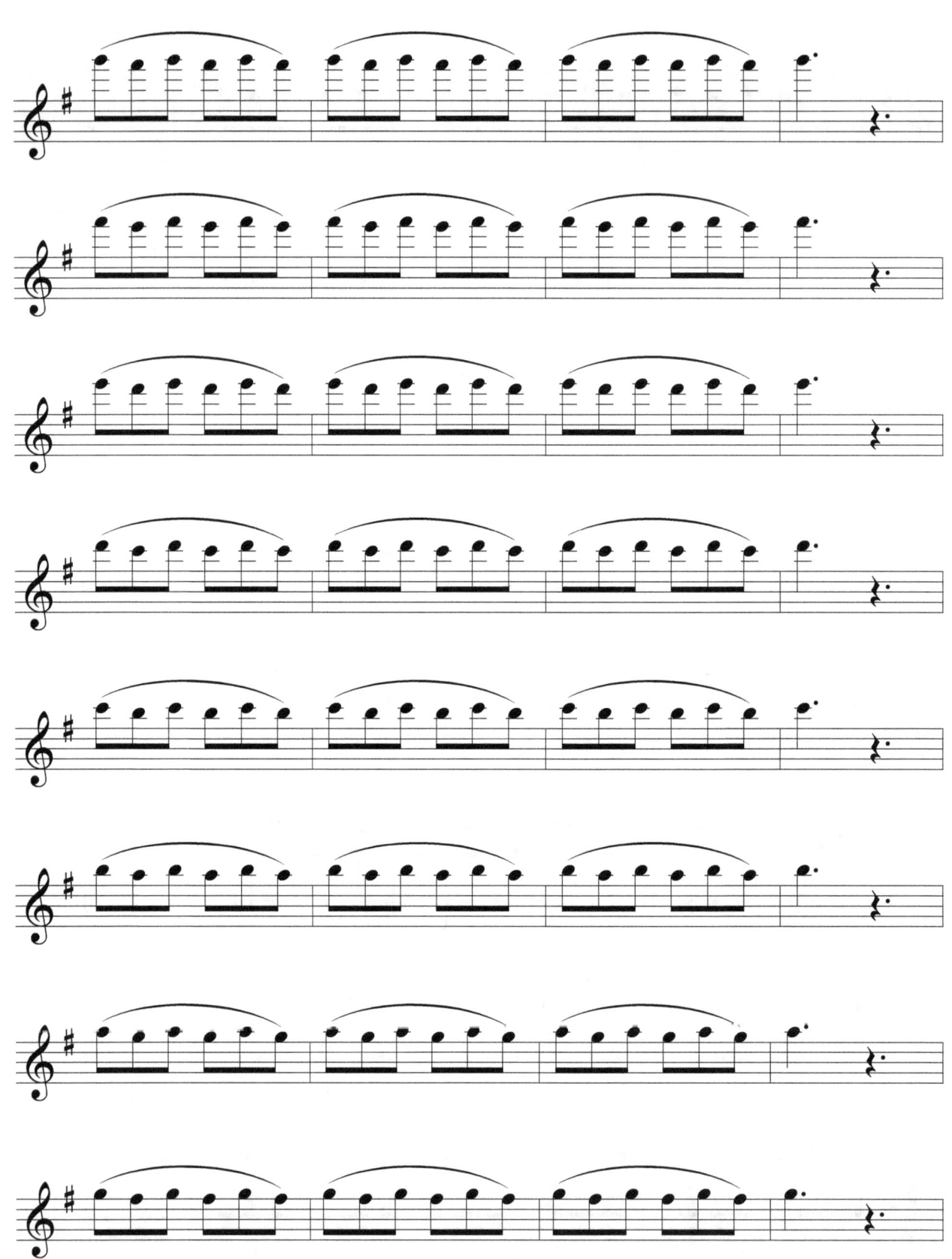

Nine-eight fine finger movement

This exercise brings together two lines from the previous exercise to create a real challenge for your fingers. Notice that it commences on low C to incorporate the bottom notes of the flute and extends up to top C to really get you working over the entire range. If you have a B foot then go all the way down there as well. Remember to play this exercise in every major and minor key.

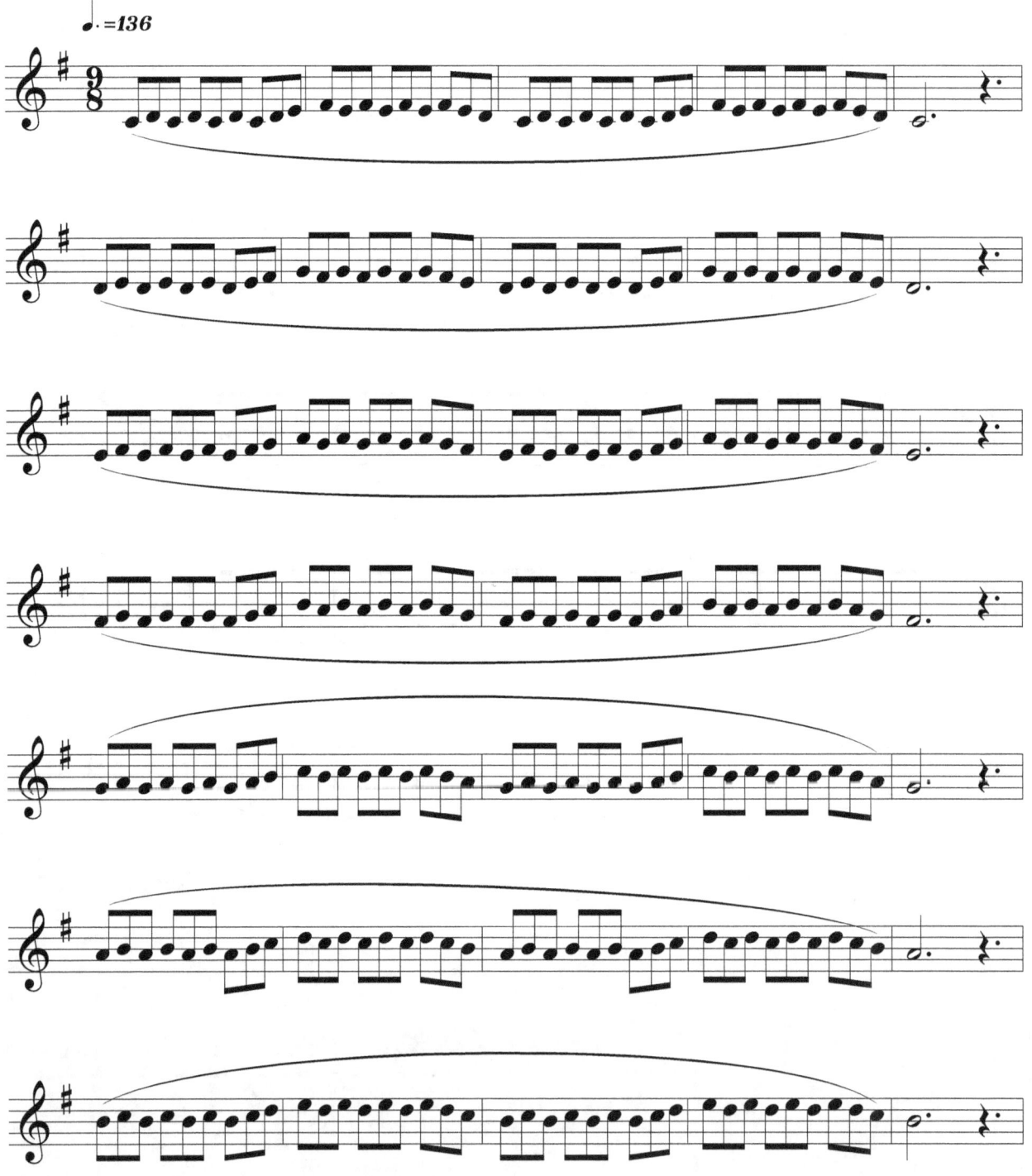

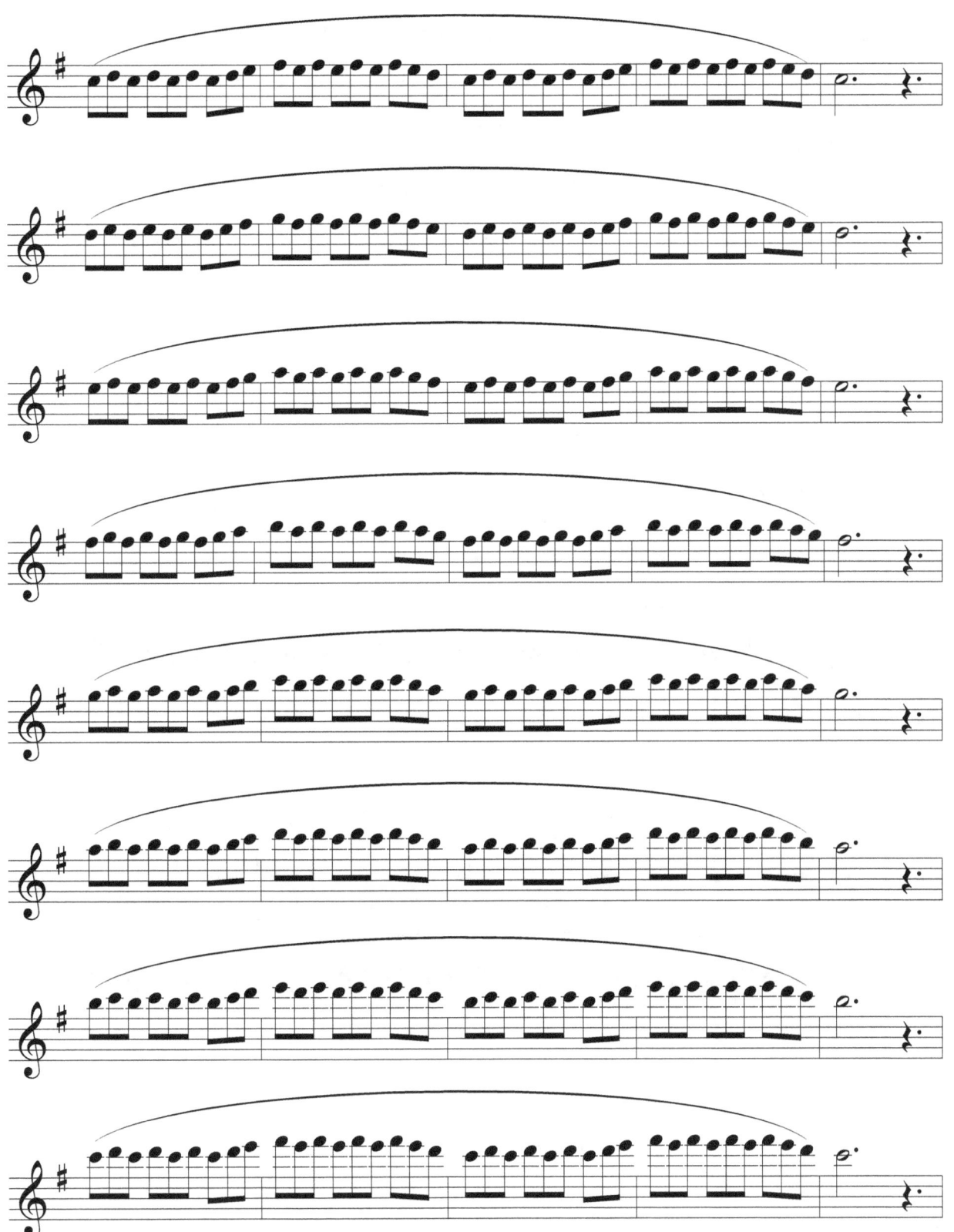

Scales 43

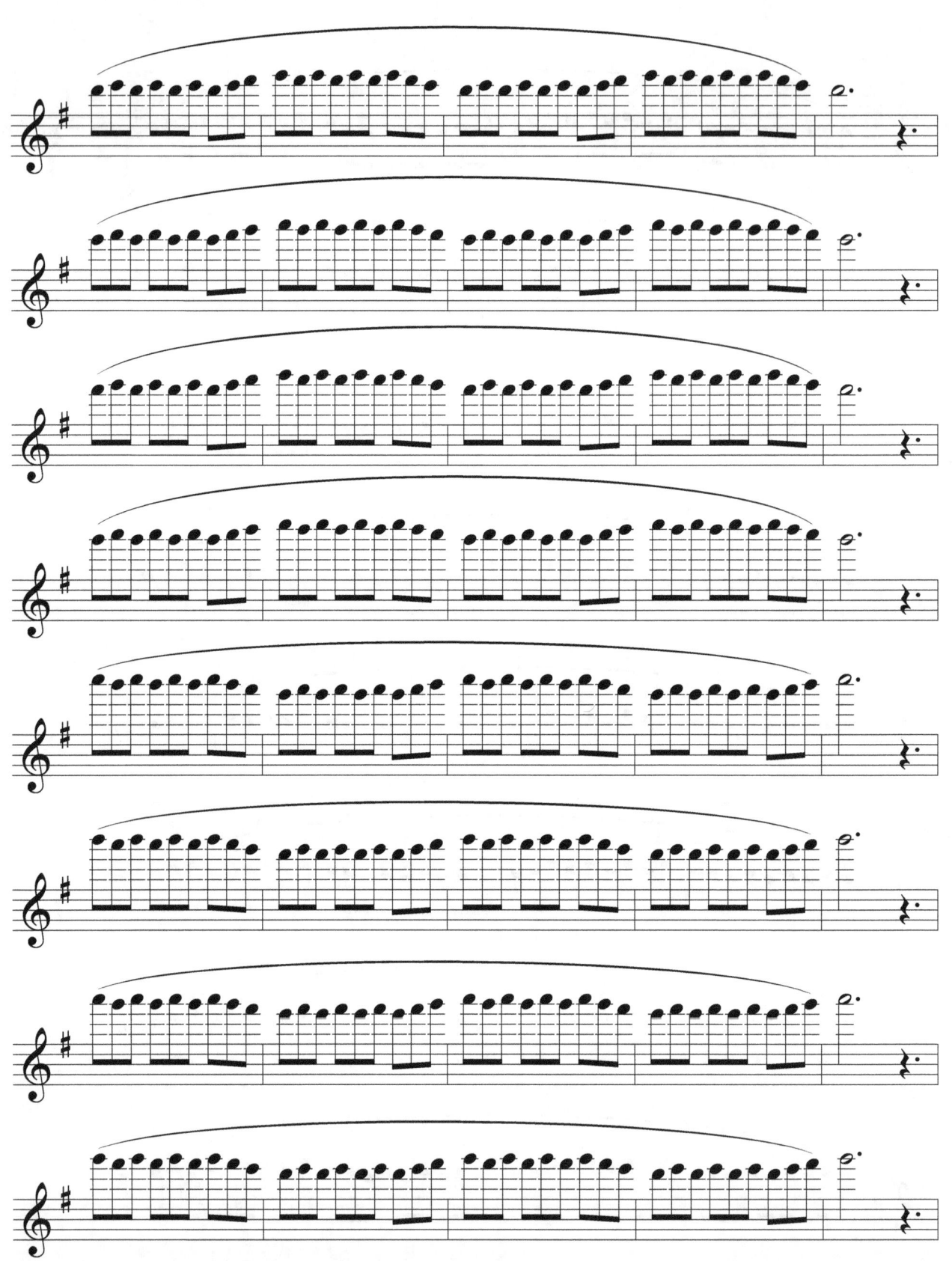

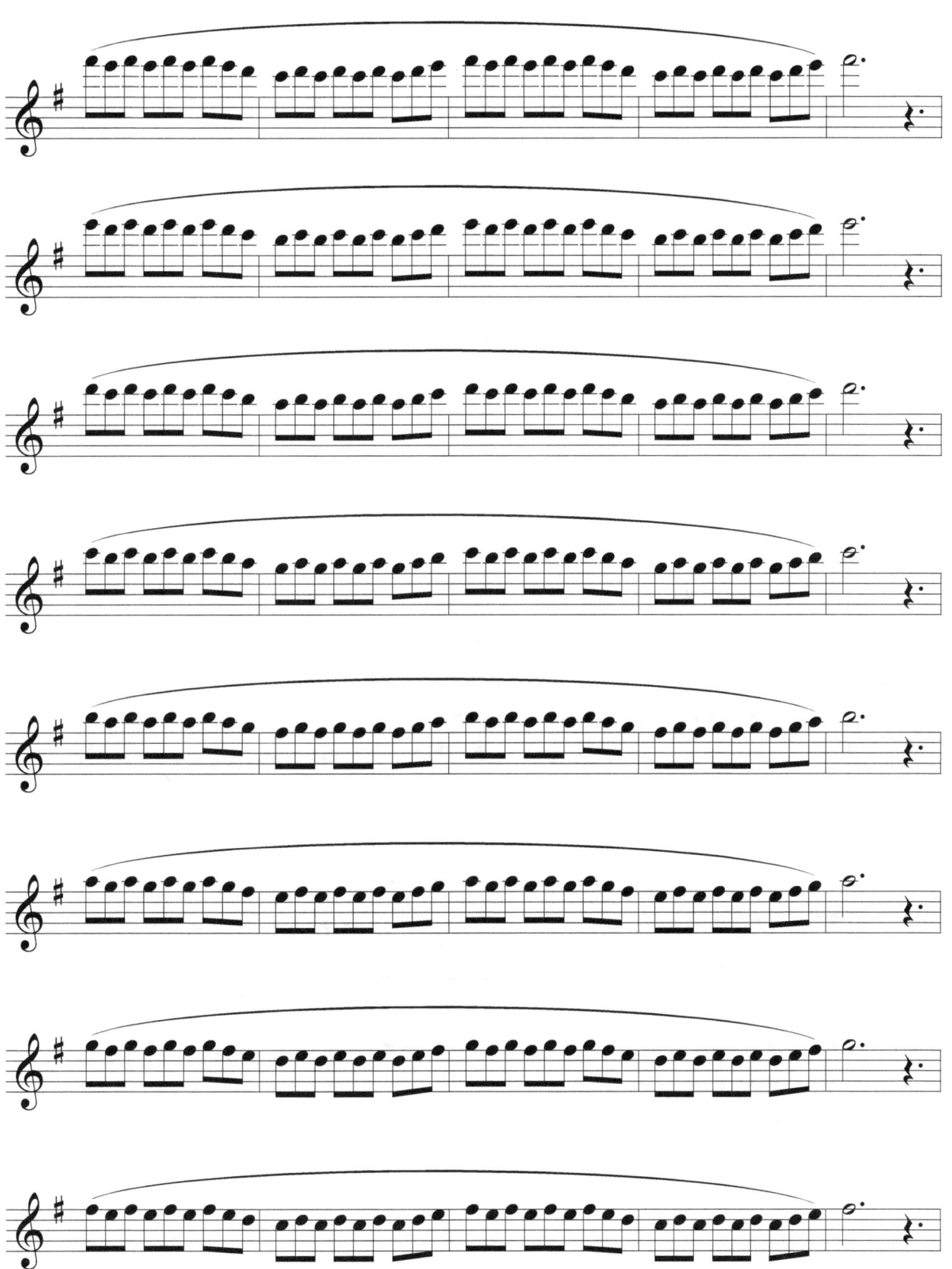

46 Supercharge Your Flute Technique

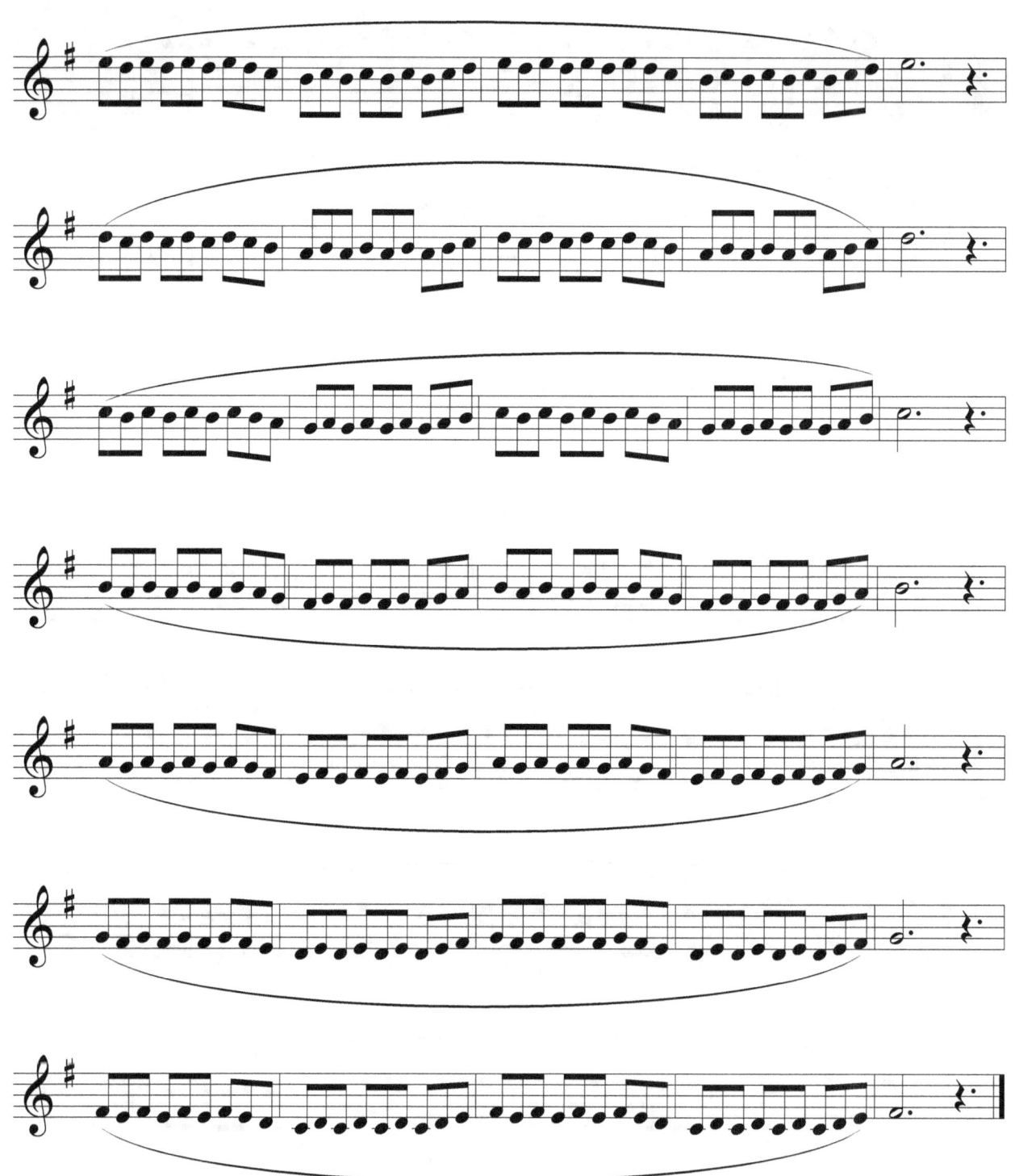

©Peter Bartels 2017
peterbartelsflute.com

Fibonacci scale

This is one of my all time favourite exercises. I've named it a Fibonacci Scale after the Italian mathematician who created the number sequence that adds the two previous numbers together; 1,2,3,5,8 and so on. Here it is given over a range of two octaves but again, feel free to extend or reduce the range to suit your level of playing

Simplified fibonacci scale

If you keep getting lost in the previous fibonacci scale try this exercise below which gets to the essence of a fibonacci scale. If you have sung in a choir this pattern may be familiar to you as a common vocal warm-up exercise.

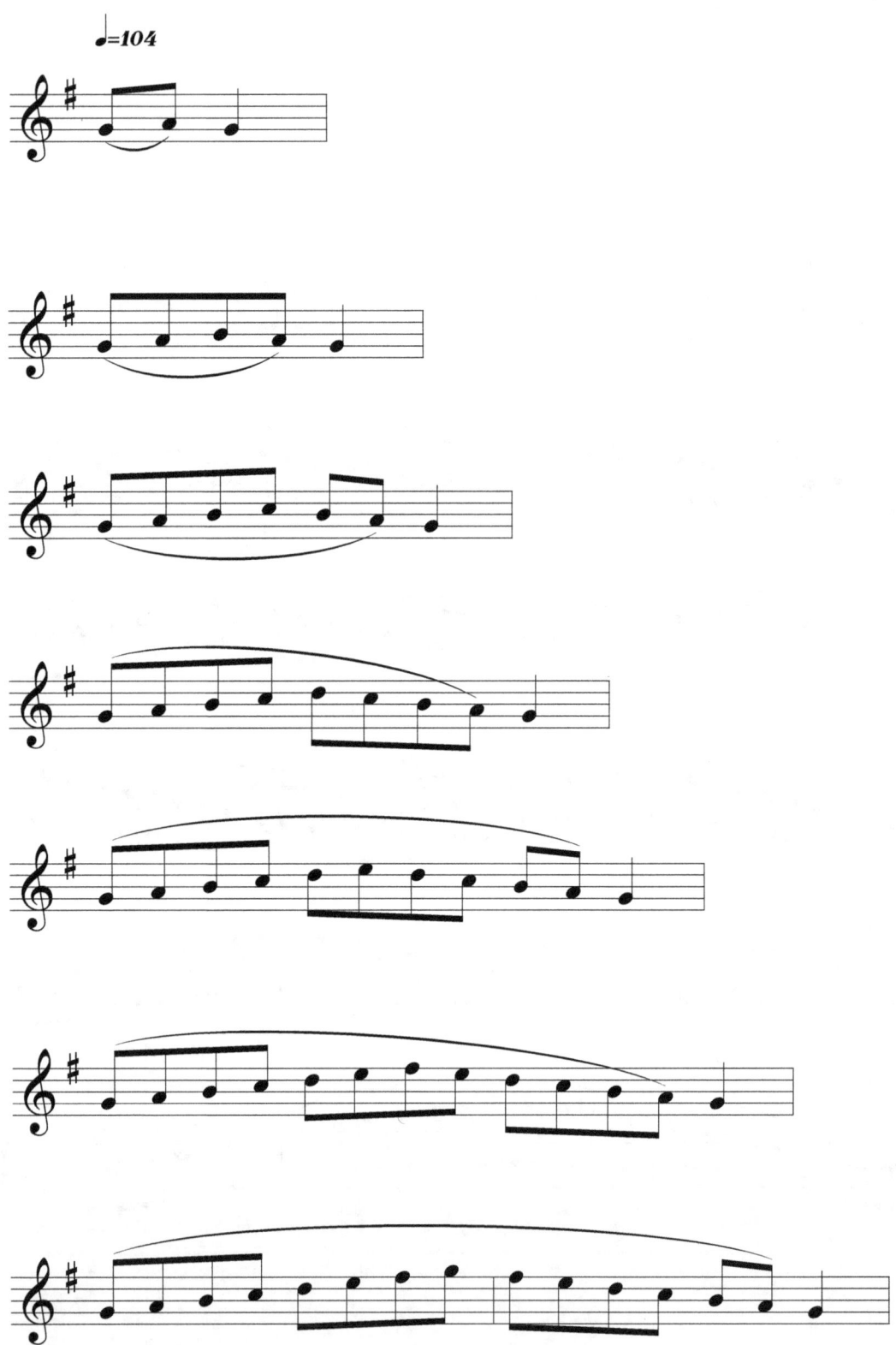

Building a scale from the top

Here is an exercise that builds up a scale starting with the top note and adding on. It is very good for reinforcing the top notes of any scale and excellent for clarifying the top part of melodic minor scales.

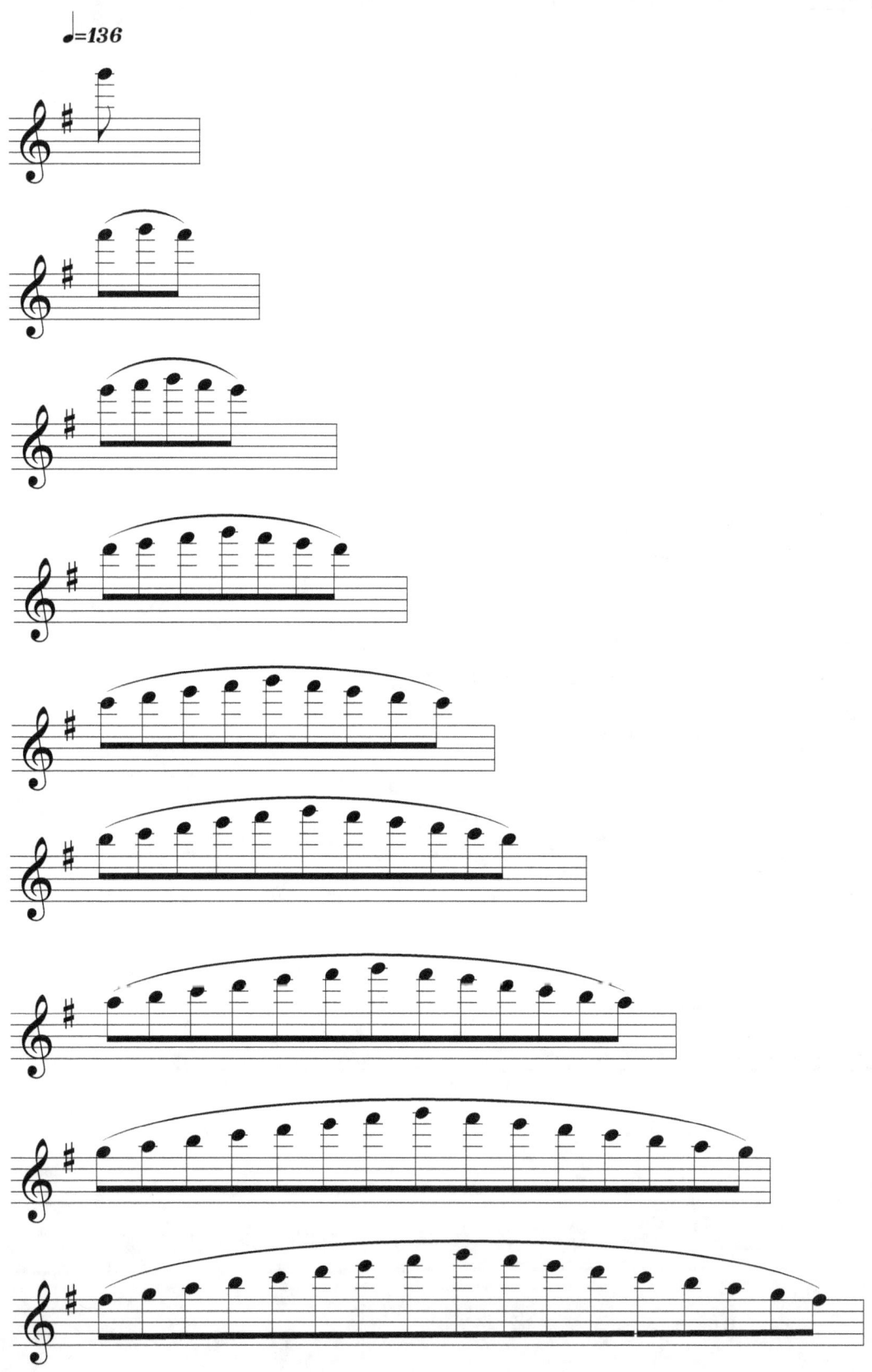

Scales 51

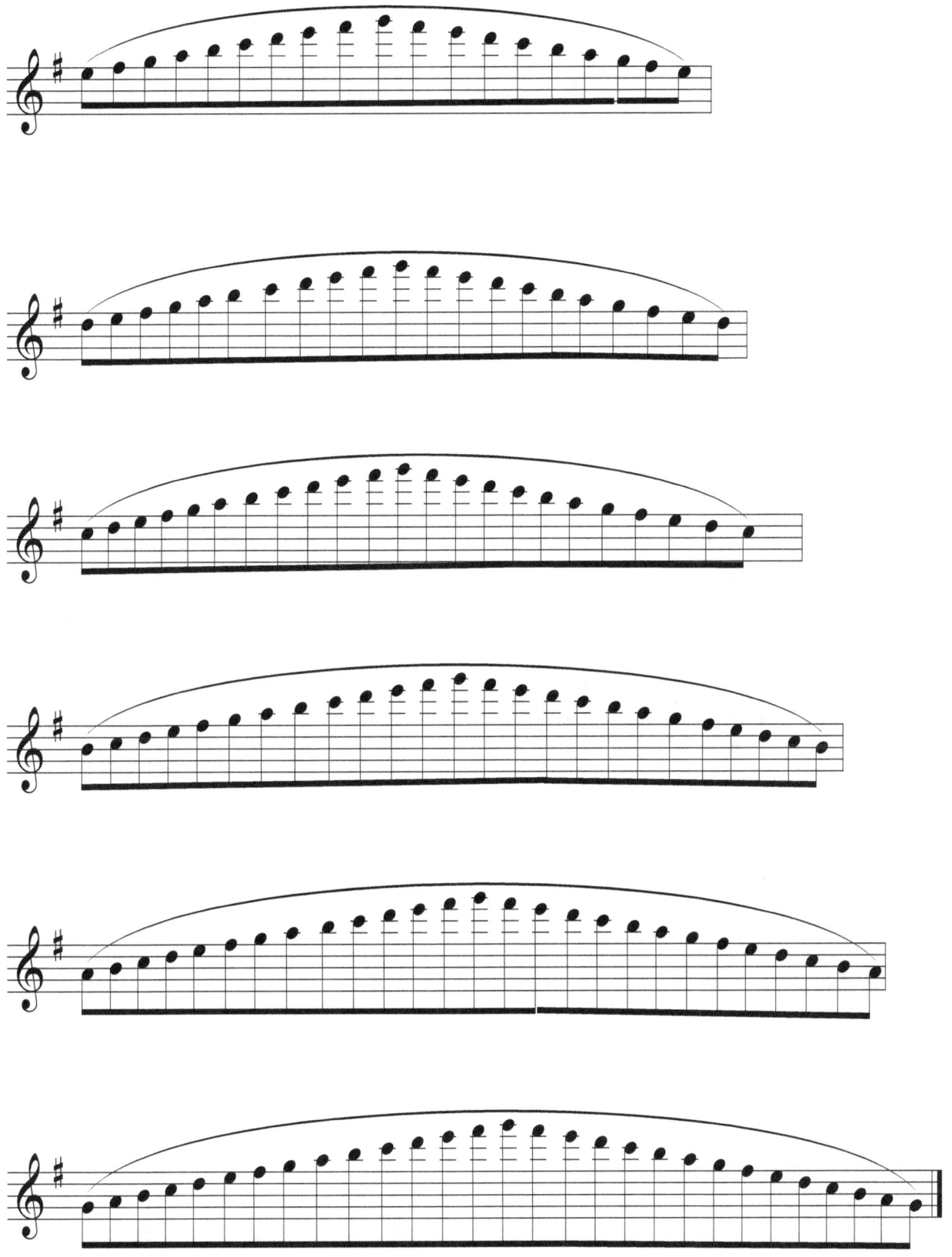

Whole tone scales

There are more varieties of scales in the big wide world than just majors and minors. It is very easy to apply the exercises in this chapter to any scales that you would like to learn.

As an example, flutes are called upon to play a lot of whole tone scales so it's worth including them in your technical practice. Remember that essentially there are only two whole tone scales in the whole wide world. Once you've learnt them on C and C# the remaining scales are just inversions. The scale on D is the C scale starting on the second note and the scale on D# is the C# scale commencing on the second note and onward the pattern goes. Learn two and you have got the lot. For the C scale I think to myself natural-natural-natural, sharp-sharp-sharp and for the C# scale I think sharp-sharp, natural-natural-natural-natural. Try them starting on every note using a variety of articulation patterns and eventually extend the range over the entire flute

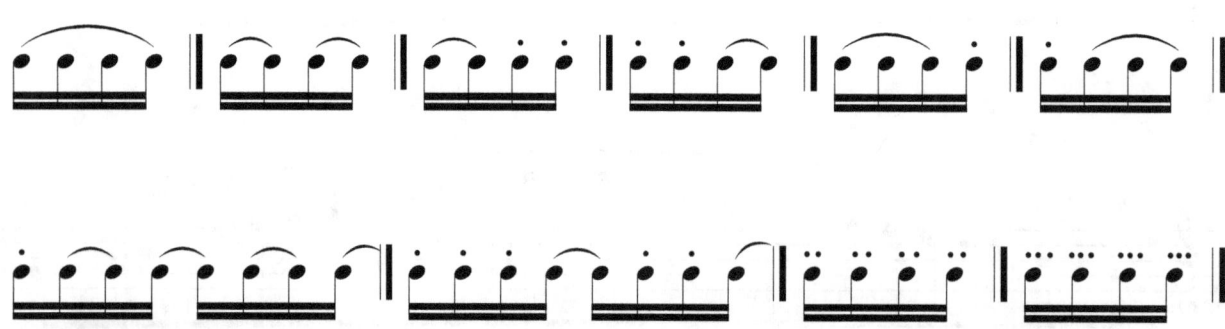

Arpeggios and broken chords

Building an arpeggio

This chapter focuses on arpeggios and broken chords. Remember to play the exercises in all major and minor keys extending or reducing the range as required. The first exercise builds up an arpeggio note by note. Put your metronome on to keep it nice and rhythmic.

©Peter Bartels 2017
peterbartelsflute.com

Arpeggios and broken chords 55

Repeating intervals

This is a good exercise for consolidating the notes in an arpeggio by repeating the intervals.

Arpeggio in three-eight

A straight forward three-eight exercise to consolidate the intervals of the arpeggio.

Arpeggios by threes

The three variations of this three-eight exercise use a triplet in every bar to emphasis each interval of the arpeggio. In variation two and three the triplet is shunted across by a beat to change the emphasis. Be sure to play the three variations in every single major and minor key.

Variation One

Variation Two

Variation Three

Breaking up broken chords

It can really help if you break your broken chords up into smaller manageable parts. This exercise takes the G major broken chord and works on each of the inversions separately.

Semiquaver broken chords

See if you can cope with this one. It is similar to the previous exercise but more intense. Play it in every major and minor key and even extend the range with one more inversion beyond the tonic at the top and the bottom where possible.

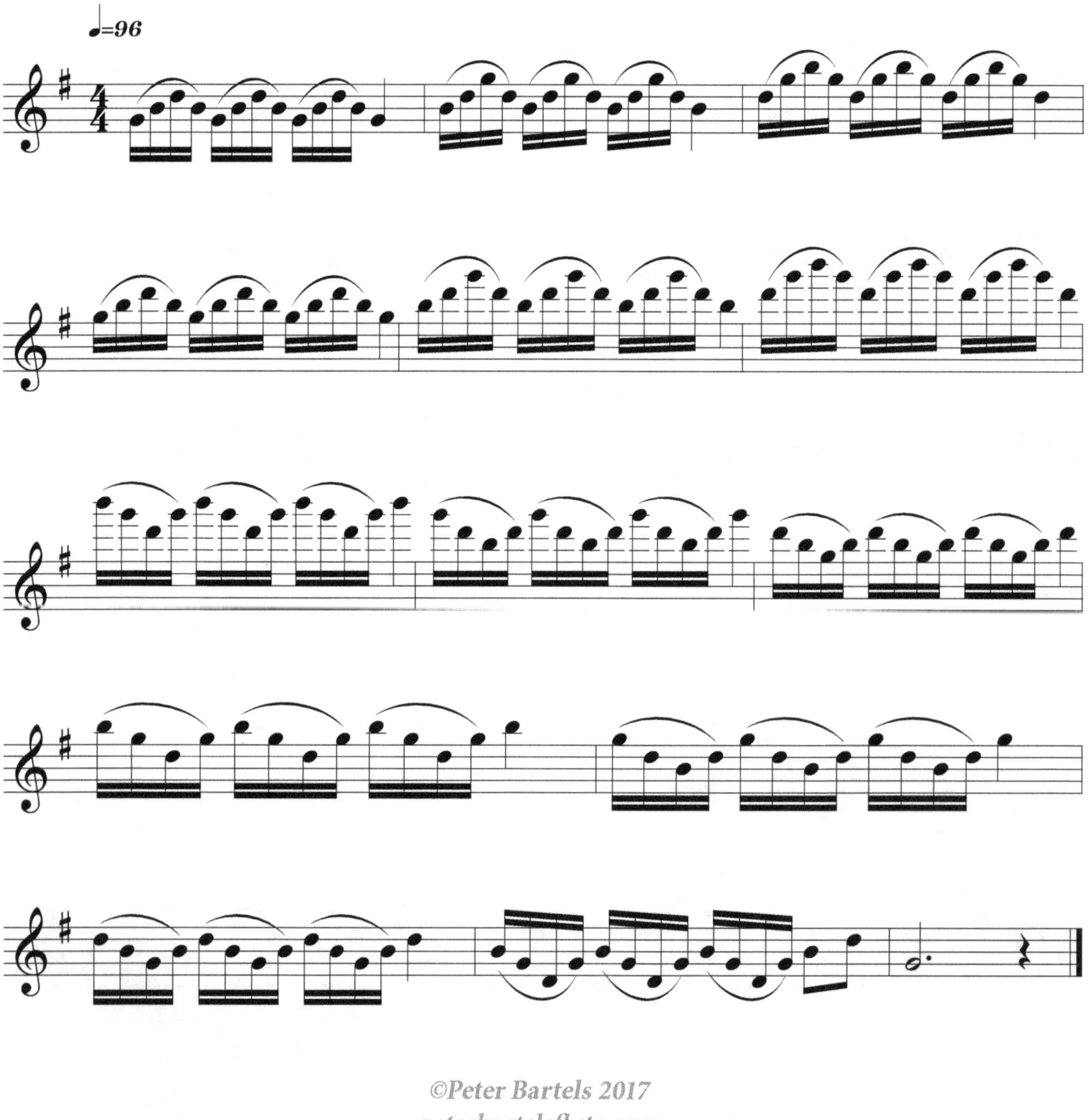

Continuously expanding arpeggio

Similar to the very first first exercise in the chapter, this exercise builds the arpeggio note by note but removes the rests. You can easily make this more challenging by extending it over the entire range. Go right up to the top B or even D and then go all the way down to low D as well or B if you have a B footjoint. That will really test you out.

Diminished arpeggios and broken chords

Up to this point the examples in this chapter have used G major as the template key. Of course all these exercises should be practised in all major and minor keys. Beyond that they can also be used for diminished arpeggios and seventh chords as well. Use the given template but alter the chord you are working on.

There are really only three diminished triads in the world. Everything beyond these three is simply an inversion or extension of those three basic chords. Below are three diminished on C, C# or D. If we were to go one semitone higher to the next diminished chord starting on D#/E♭, that is simply the first inversion of the C diminished chord and so on it goes. So you only need to learn these three arpeggios and their enharmonic equivalent and you will have conquered diminished arpeggios.

Diminished 7th arpeggios

Here are the diminished 7th arpeggios written out to help you along the way. Remember that diminished 7th arpeggios are just a pile of minor thirds. I think of them as Greensleeves on Greensleeves on Greensleeves on Greensleeves. Notice that every fourth line is just an inversion of what has gone before. The exercise is written with two slurred, two tongued but go wild and try these arpeggios out with a wide variety of articulation patterns.

Dominant 7th arpeggios and broken chords

And a final word regarding dominant 7th arpeggios and broken chords. Simply go back and apply the same exercise templates in this chapter to all your dominant 7th chords. Be creative and ensure that you are covering every single key with a variety of articulation patterns and of course using your metronome to keep things even and steady. And a tip for working out the 7th note is to remember that it is a whole tone below the upper tonic and not just a semitone like a leading note.

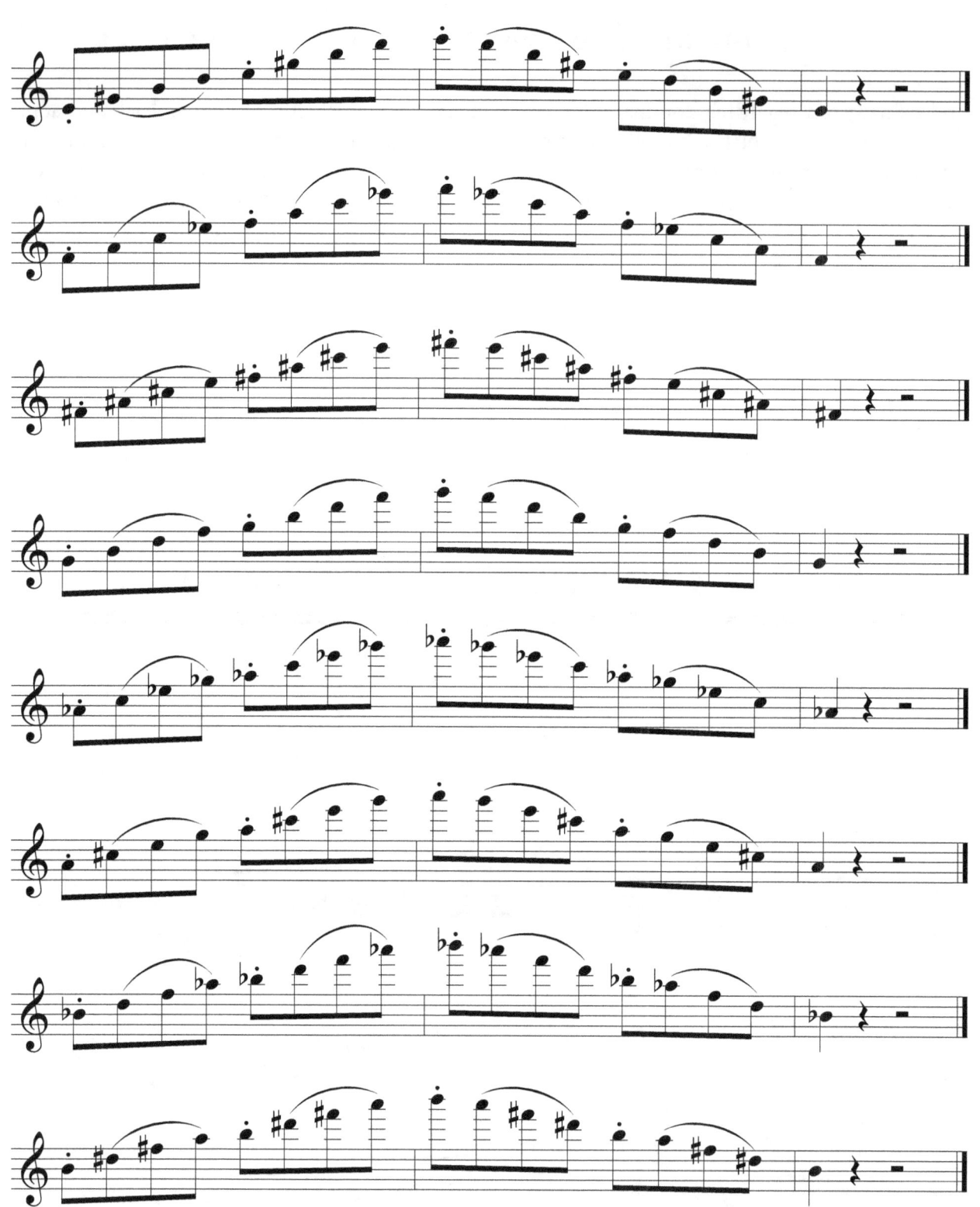

Chromatics

Chromatic corners

Fast and even chromatic runs sound impressive, magical and fantastic on the flute so it is really worth the effort required to get them sounding great. I also think they are a clear indicator of the health of your technique. Good chromatics are a harbinger of good technique. This first exercise, chromatic corners, is aimed at exploring the concept of chromatic neighbour notes. Remember that the often under utilised B♭ lever key can be very helpful when ascending in chromatics. You can put it on nice and early as a preparation for the approaching B♭/A♯.

Climbing chromatics

The next exercise starts working the chromatics into groups, which will become the basis for a lot of further work on chromatics. Approach your chromatics from a rhythmic perspective rather than notes. By that I mean feel the rhythm very strongly and then you won't go too far with your chromatic scales, you just stop at the appropriate beat rather than the appropriate note.

Repeated semiquaver blocks

Now to really start getting those fingers moving here is an exercise to work with those previously mentioned blocks. This exercise focuses on the three, four note groups that are in each octave of a chromatic scale. The repeats are written out but really you should keep working on each group until it sounds absolutely fantastic; super even and smooth.

©Peter Bartels 2017
peterbartelsflute.com

Chromatic Scales

Pausing on the beat

Following on with the groups in the previous exercise, here is a chromatic scale broken down into those semiquaver blocks.

Pausing at the octave

Now try the same idea of working in groups but put three groups together to form each octave of your scale.

©Peter Bartels 2017
peterbartelsflute.com

Pillar notes

Try the following exercise to really get those fingers whizzing along on your chromatic scales. It still uses the concept of breaking a chromatic down into semiquaver blocks however there is no rest between the ascent and descent on each group. It's a tough exercise and you will really need to concentrate, but it is fabulous fun.

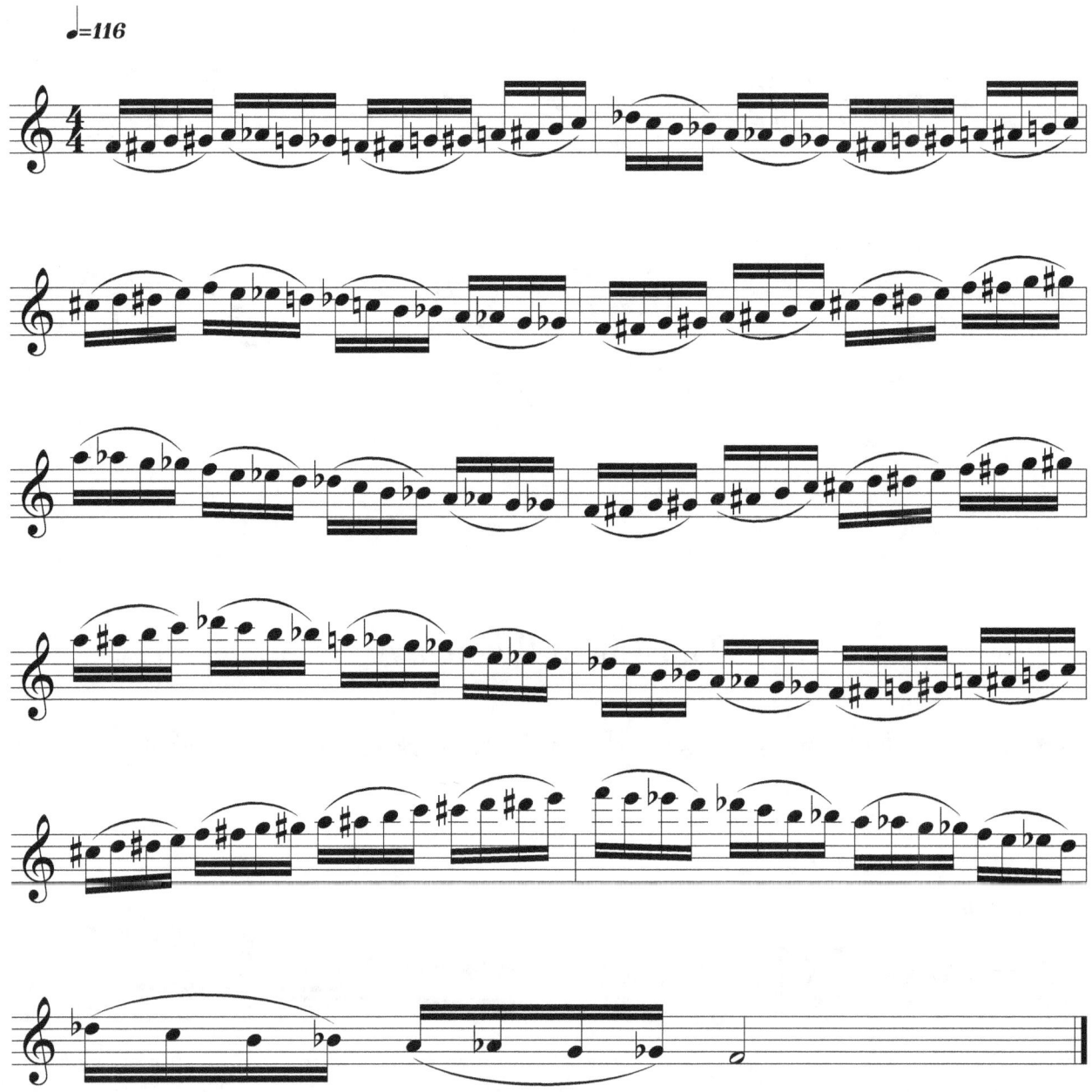

The four augmented triads

So far in this chapter the exercises have been based on a chromatic starting on F. Of course you should now go back and learn to play each exercise starting on every pitch. You will notice by doing this that the pillar notes of each chromatic, if they are grouped in fours, are always based on an augmented triad. So the pillar notes for the F chromatic are F, A and C♯. If you invert this triad you will realise that the chromatic commencing on A has the same pillar notes as the chromatic on F, just moving one block higher. Likewise for C♯, which will start one block lower than F. Since there are essentially only four augmented triads in the world, before they start inverting, you really only have to learn four chromatics in order to play all your chromatics well. Just know the pillar notes of the chromatic you are about to play before you begin, then base your chromatic in solid rhythm and you'll be amazed at the results. Make friends with your metronome!

At this point it would be prudent to go back and try the hitherto chromatic exercises with the following articulation patterns.

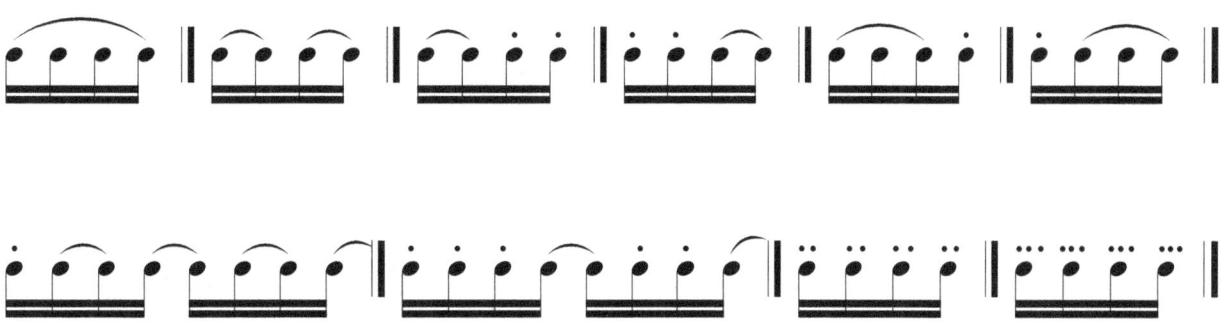

©Peter Bartels 2017
peterbartelsflute.com

Octave leaps

The next few exercises start to move away from just being based on F. This octave leaps exercise gets you working from every pitch within the F chromatic scale.

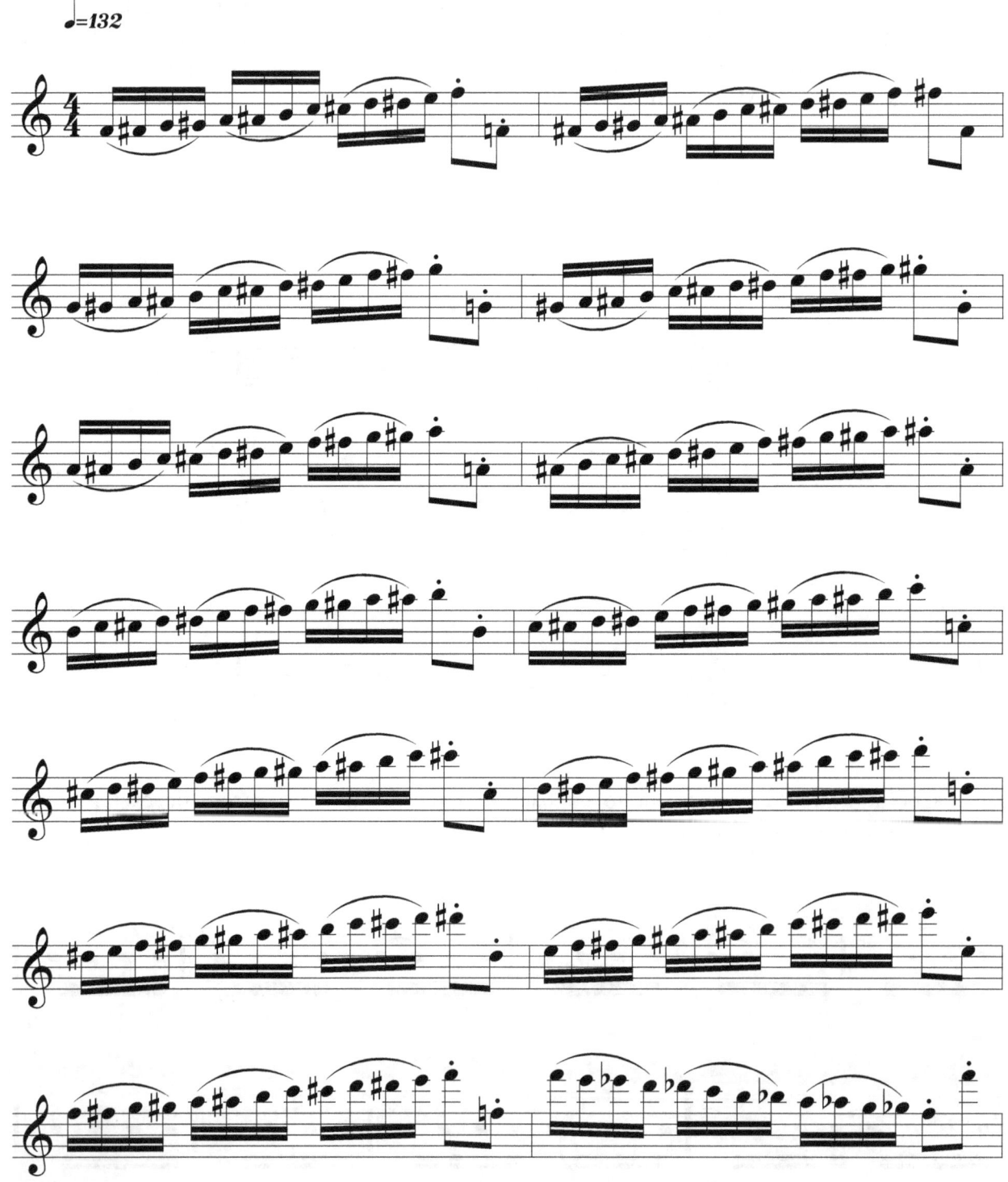

Chromatic Scales

Tied up nine-eight chromatic

The following two exercises use compound time signatures instead of duple time signatures. The first, in nine-eight, is really a preparatory exercise for the second challenging six-eight exercise. Be sure to come off the tied note very accurately. Use your metronome and feel the tied note in your soul!

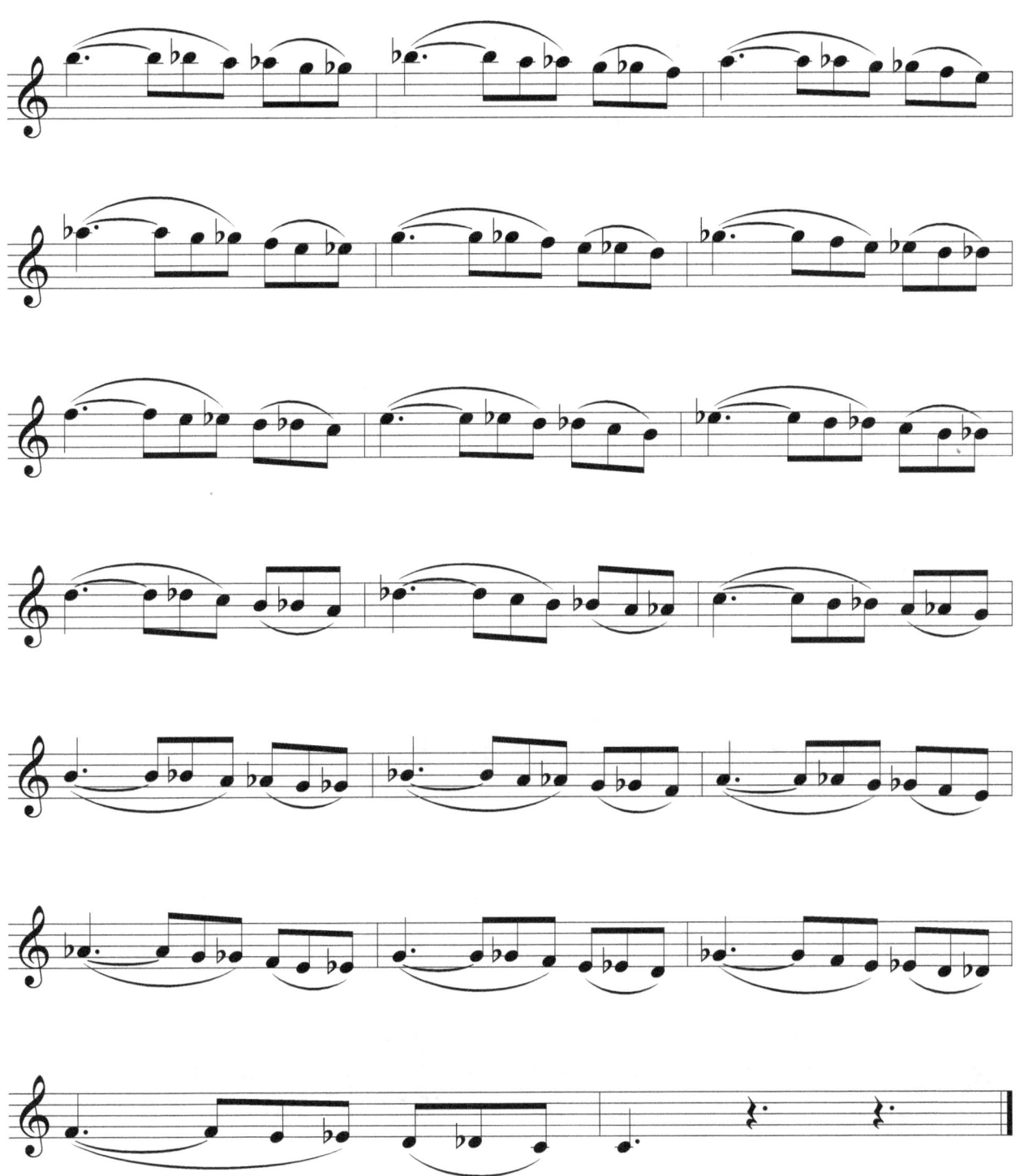

Six-eight chromatic by step

Good luck! Just focus on the first note of each bar moving chromatically by step and let the rhythm do the rest.

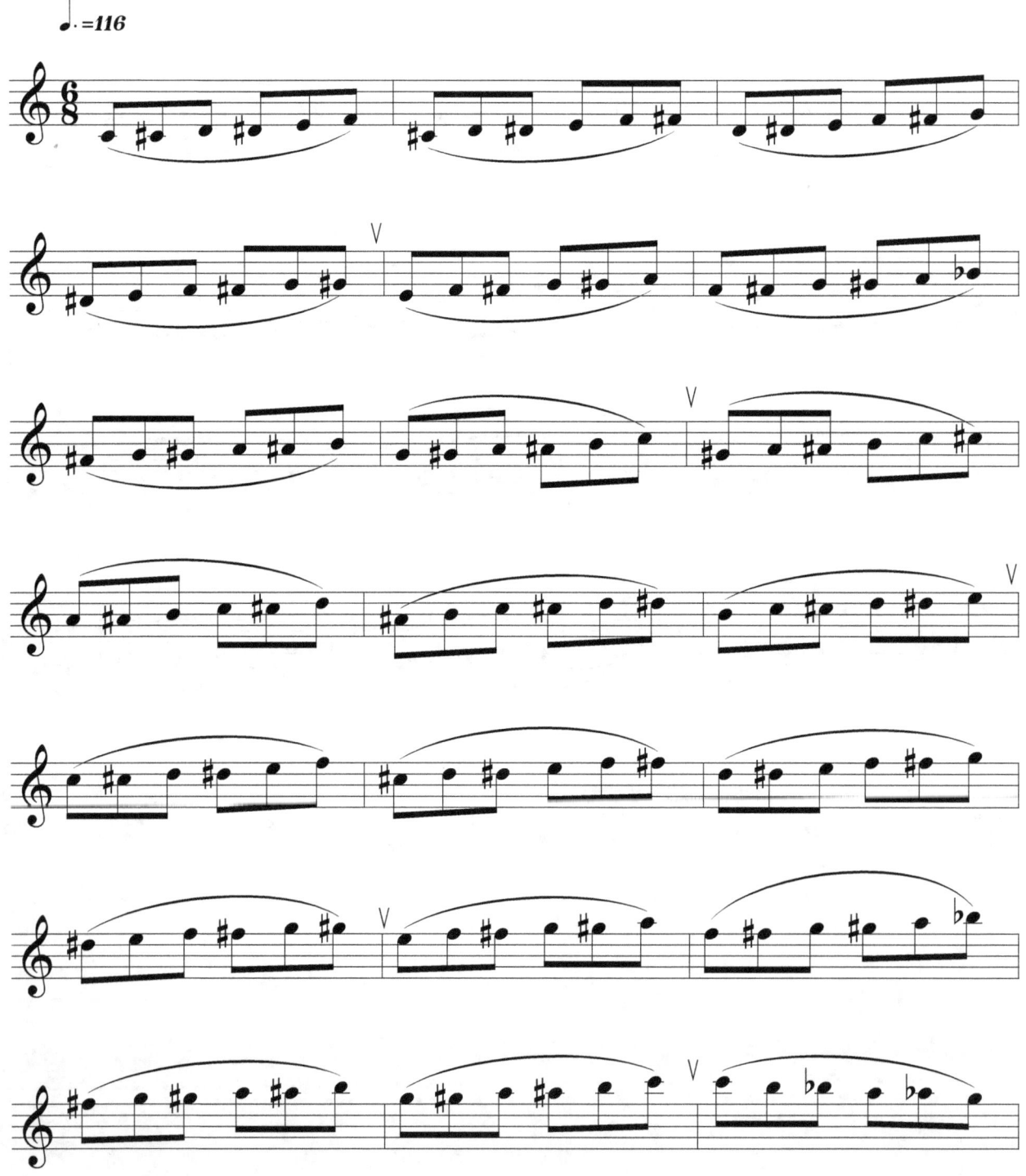

Chromatic Scales 81

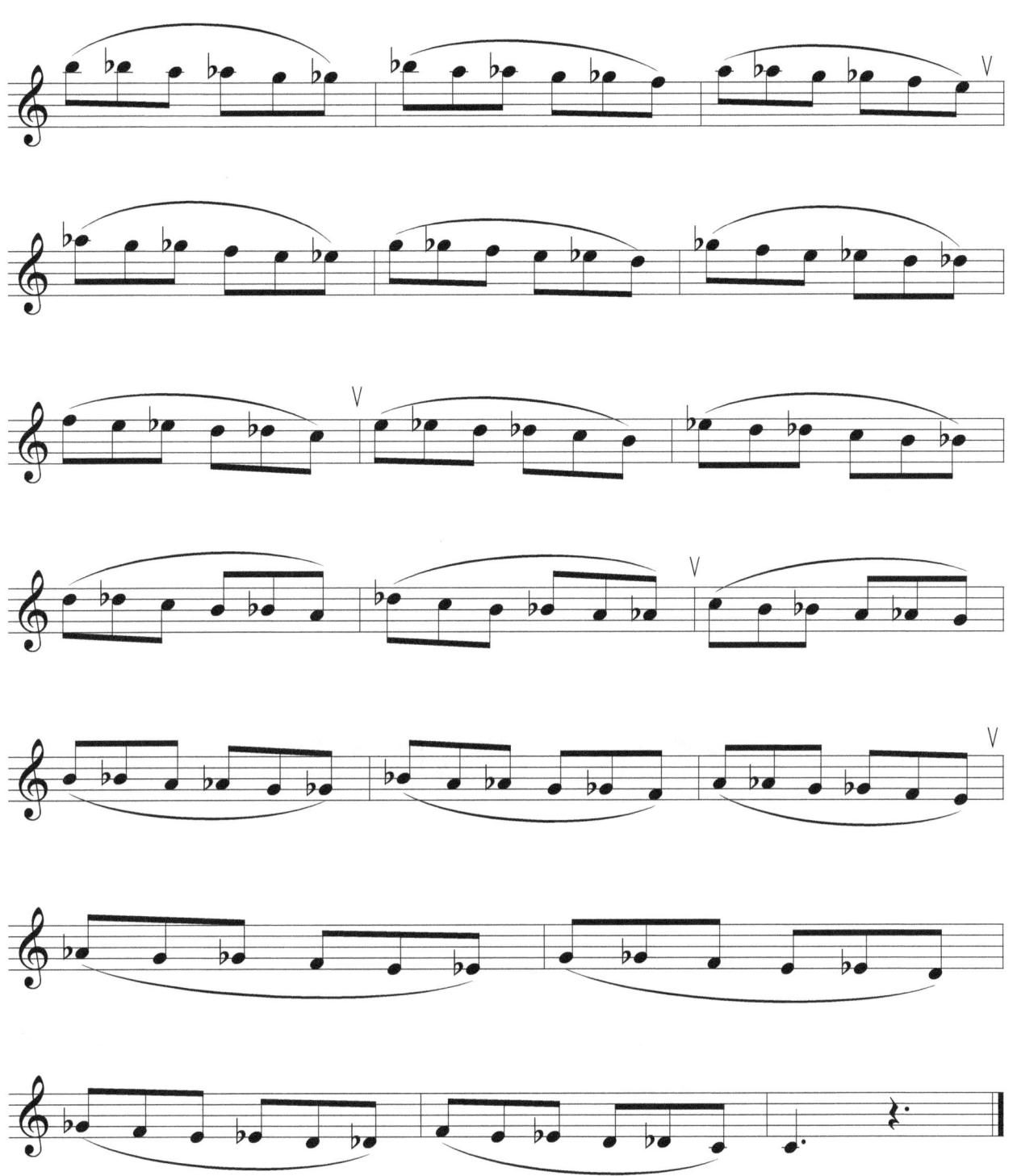

Scales in thirds

Rising and descending thirds

Let's begin our exploration of scales in thirds with this simple first exercise that introduces the concept of jumping a third and then moving by a step. Try it out in lots of different keys.

Thirds in three four

Here is an exercise in triple time which once again reinforces the intervals of a scale in thirds. You could omit the bars containing the minims to make the exercise more continuous and therefore more challenging.

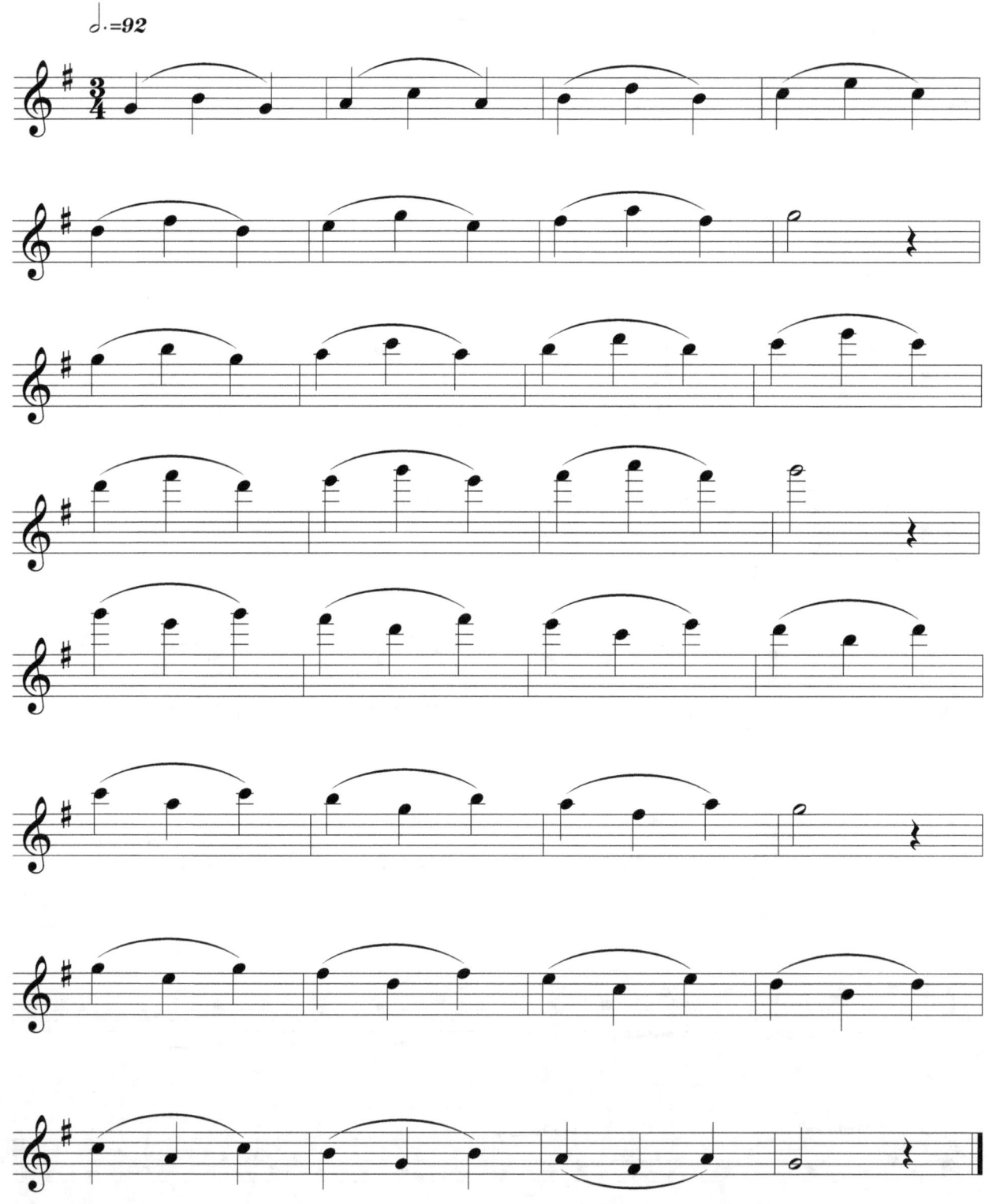

Manageable blocks by step

The following two exercises break the scale in thirds into smaller, manageable blocks. The first exercise moves by step, bar for bar, but the second exercise puts the ascending block and the corresponding descending block adjacent to each other.

Manageable blocks ascending and descending

Scales in thirds

Looping around

Now try this more challenging exercise which links up the small segments from the previous two exercises. Repeat each two bar loop as many times as you like to get it flowing before moving onto to the next loop. And of course extend the range if you want that extra challenge.

©Peter Bartels 2017
peterbartelsflute.com

Building up your scales in thirds

Practice the lower octave of a scale in thirds.

Now play the second octave of the same scale in thirds.

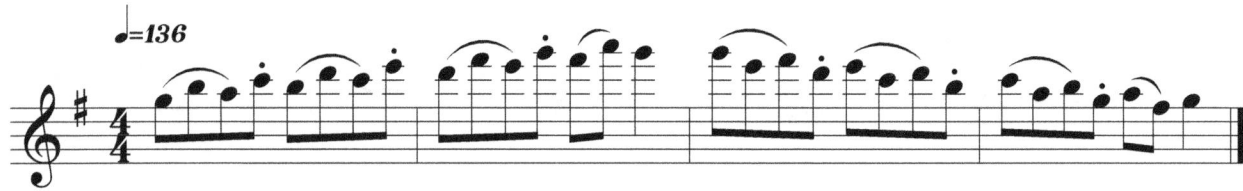

Join the previous two octaves together to create a scale in thirds stopping at each occurrence of the tonic.

And finally play the two octave scale in thirds without stopping.

Scales in thirds over the entire range

For a greater technical challenge extend your scales in thirds over the entire range. You can choose what your top note will be. Perhaps start with the top B and then extend up further as your technique develops. Play down to low C or C# in the bottom register or even low B if you have a B footjoint.

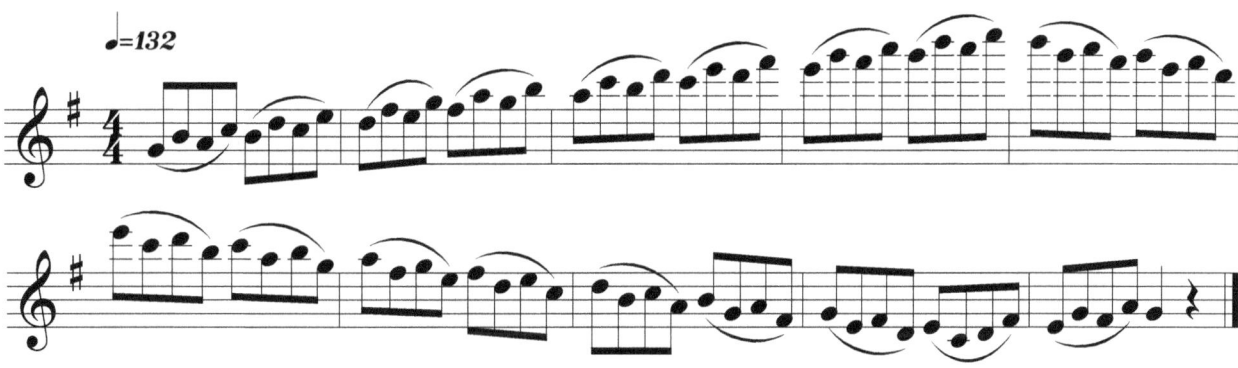

Often it is the very top of the scale that causes problems so isolate the third register notes and repeat this top portion of the scale until it becomes beautifully fluent.

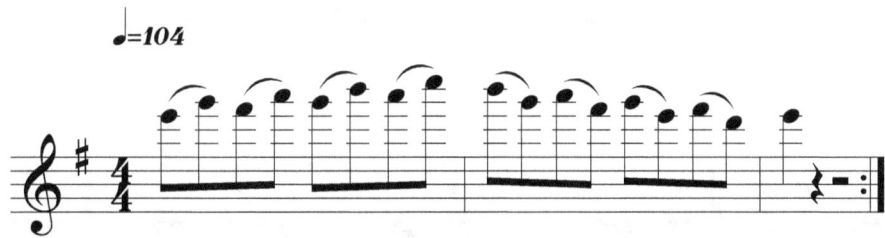

The same applies to the bottom of the scale. Start in all keys at the tonic and make your way downwards and return to the tonic. Repeat this lots of times as well.

©Peter Bartels 2017
peterbartelsflute.com

With all these exercises remember to work on them in every single key using a wide variety of articulation patterns.

Working on challenging passages

Using rhythms on a run

If you have a passage of constant semiquavers, altering the rhythm to emphasis different notes in that passage can be a very useful method of learning the notes and gaining fluency. As you play each rhythmic alteration, the changes on the shorter notes should be sharp and quick, taking your time on the longer notes to consolidate them and prepare for the next fast change. Below is an example of a constant semiquaver run. It is then followed by eight rhythmic alterations. Keep the dotted notes very pointed so that the little notes are very quick. Half the notes within the beat will be very fast while the other half are slower, alternating quick changes with consolidation of notes.

Pausing on each note

Instead of altering the rhythm, as in the previous exercise, the following four lines, in turn, pause on each of the semiquavers in each beat. First the fourth of each group of four semiquavers, then the third, the second and the first. Three notes will be very fast while the paused note is consolidated and gives you a chance to check out the next three notes.

After you have practised all these variations, remember to go back and play the original passage again. Hopefully it will have improved!

Rhythmic alterations in compound time

Of course not all runs are in duple time but may well be in compound time. Here is an example passage in 6/8 followed by three rhythms that could be used to help consolidate the notes and gain fluency. When working with altered rhythms remember to keep the rhythm very pointed. Exaggerate the dotted notes so that the change is very quick while the longer note is reinforced.

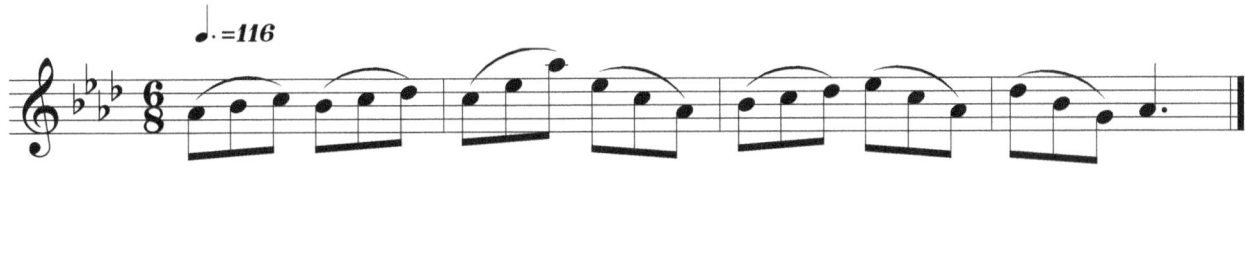

Pausing on each note in compound time

Now try pausing in turn on the third, second and first note of each dotted crotchet beat. Remember to move quickly from one pause to the next while using the moment on the pause to scan ahead for the next notes.

You can also extend the frequency of the pause. This time the pauses occur only once per bar meaning you have to play six notes rapidly before holding for a moment.

Remember to go back and play the original passage again and marvel at the improvement.

The backwards game

The backwards game is a fun way to work on a semiquaver run. In the following example, start by playing the last note. Then play the penultimate note plus the last note, then add on the third last note continuing in this fashion until you have made your way right back to the first note. I reckon if you make a mistake before reaching the last line you have to go back and start the whole exercise again.

Working on challenging passages

The forwards game

It doesn't take rocket science to work out that the forwards game is the same as the backwards game except that you commence with the first note and build from there. Remember, if you make an error on any line it's back to the start for you!

©Peter Bartels 2017
peterbartelsflute.com

Working on challenging passages

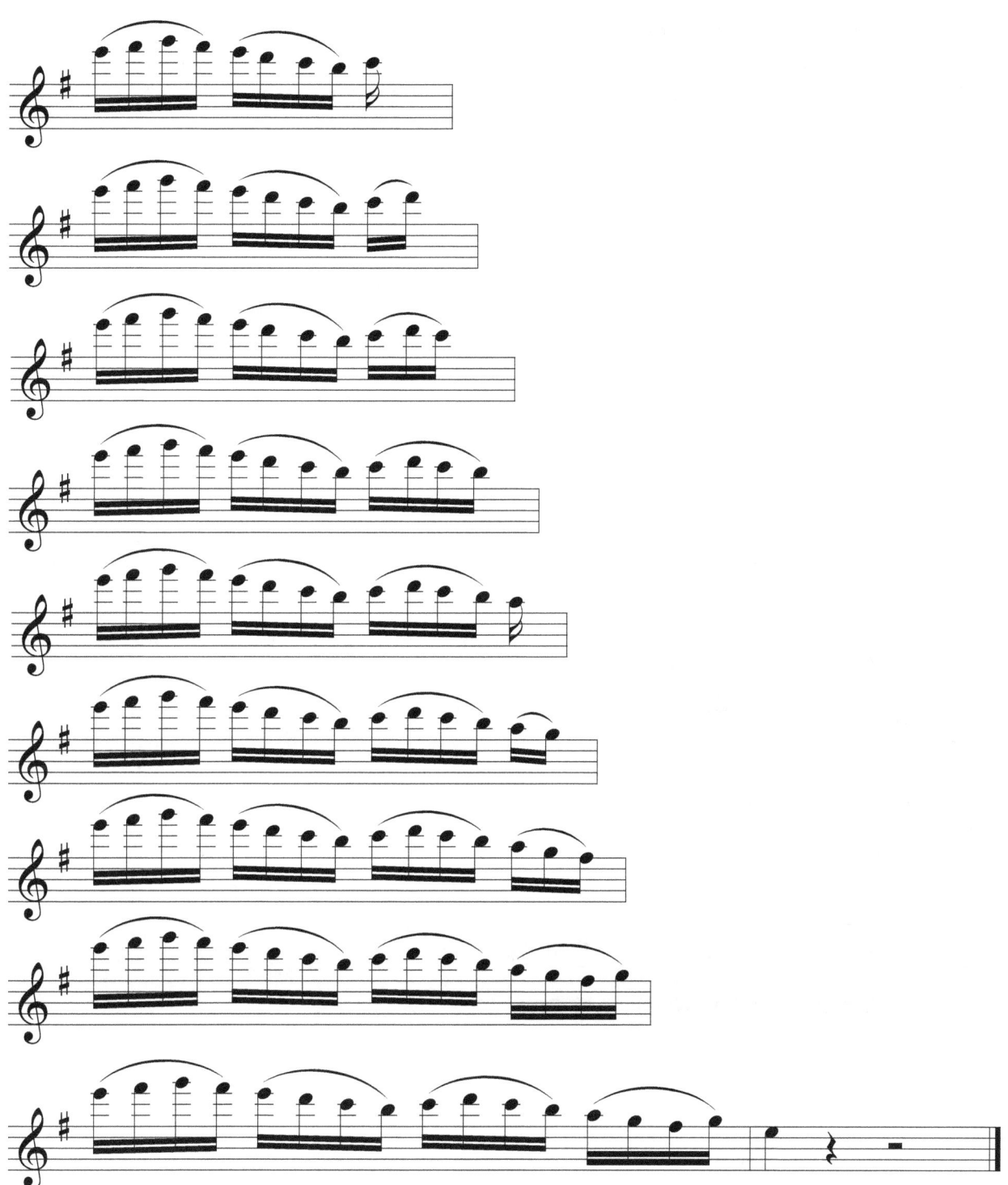

Forward fibonacci run

If you've ever sung in a choir, a very popular warm-up is to sing up and down a scale in the pattern 1, 121, 12321, 1234321 and so on. The following exercise uses that pattern to work on the run. So play 121, then 12321 and continue in this manner until you end up playing the run through forwards and then backwards returning to the start. You'll need to concentrate!

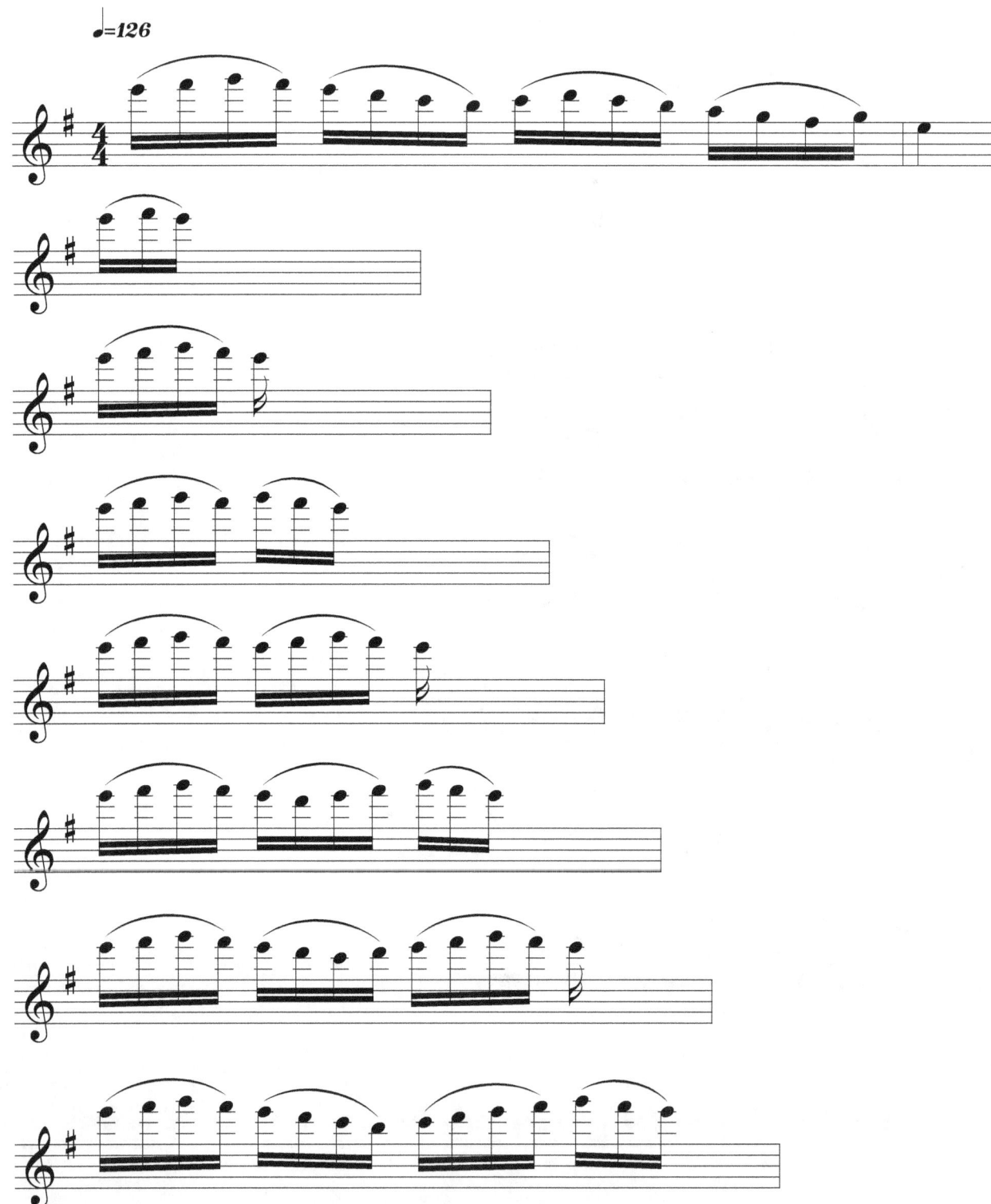

Working on challenging passages 103

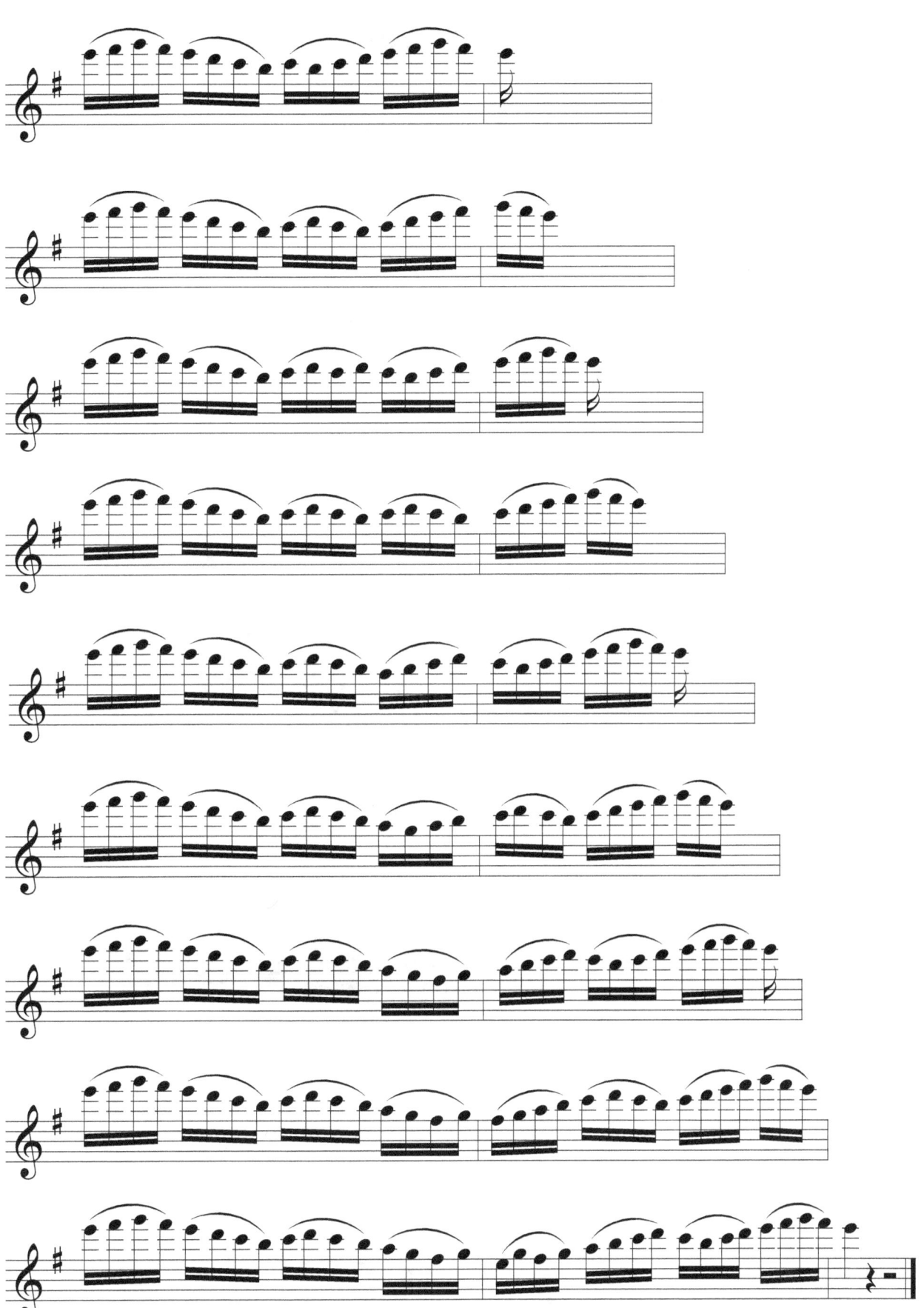

Backward fibonacci run

This exercise is the reverse of the previous forward fibonacci run. Do the same thing but commence from the end of the run. Concentrate and it's you back to the start if you make an error.

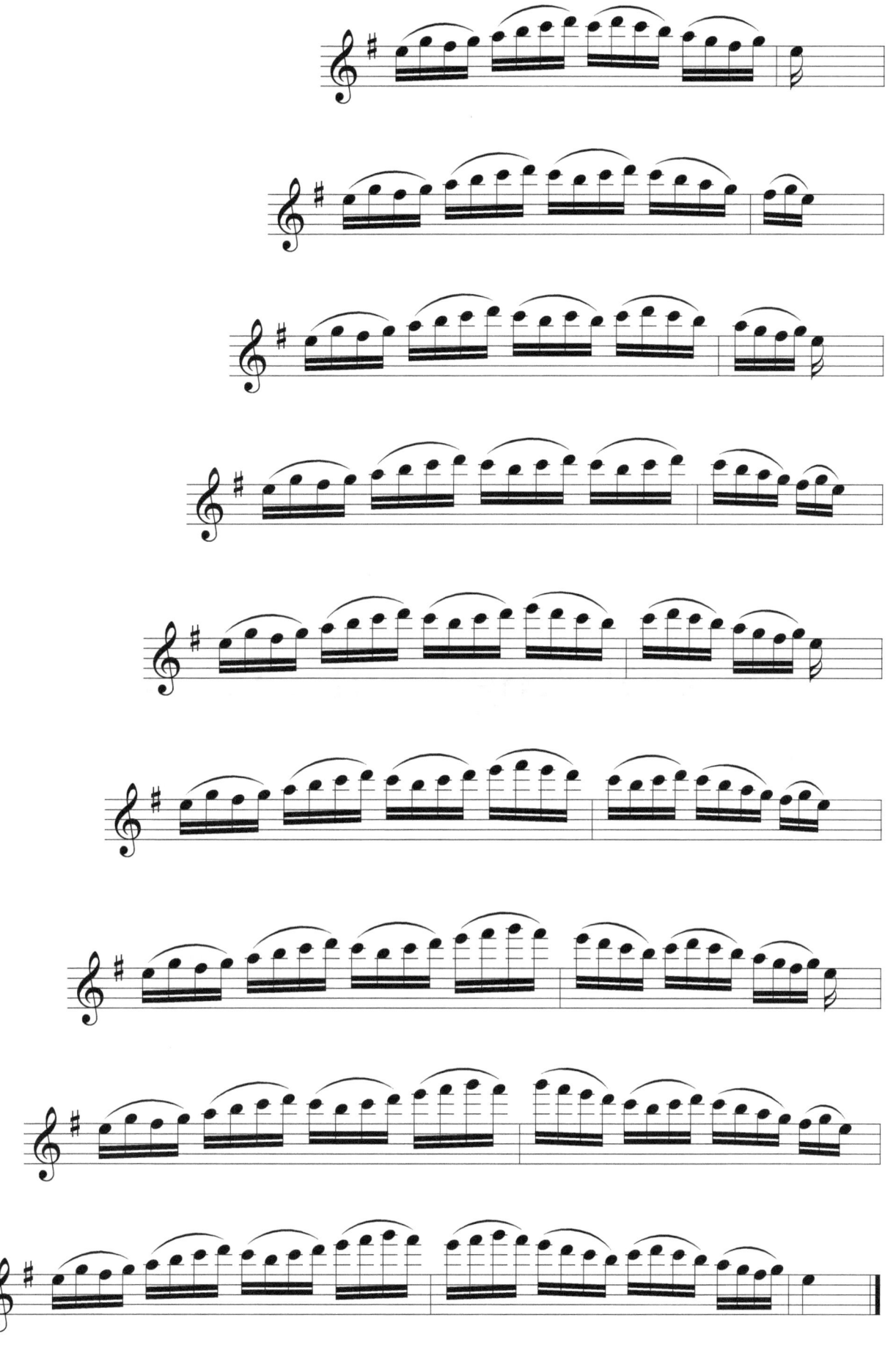

Organising your practice

Cycle of fifths

One of my favourite ways of organising my practice is to use the cycle of fifths. So whatever it is that I'm practising, I play it around the cycle. For example if I'm practising my modal scales I will start at C major and whizz around the circle. In the middle of the cycle of fifths below, I have listed some of the technical elements you might like to try out. You could take any exercise in this book and do it the same way. At the very bottom of the page is the order of sharps and flats in case you need a reminder of which one comes next. Remember that as you make your way through the sharp keys, the next new sharp added in is always the leading note of the new key. So if you're in D major, the next key is A major so the new sharp will be A major's leading note G#. Simple! With the flat keys if you're sure not of what the key is then go back one flat from the last flat in the key signature. For example, if there are two flats, B♭ and E♭, in the key signature then the key will be B♭ major (or G minor) as B♭ is one step back from the last flat in the key signature which is E♭.

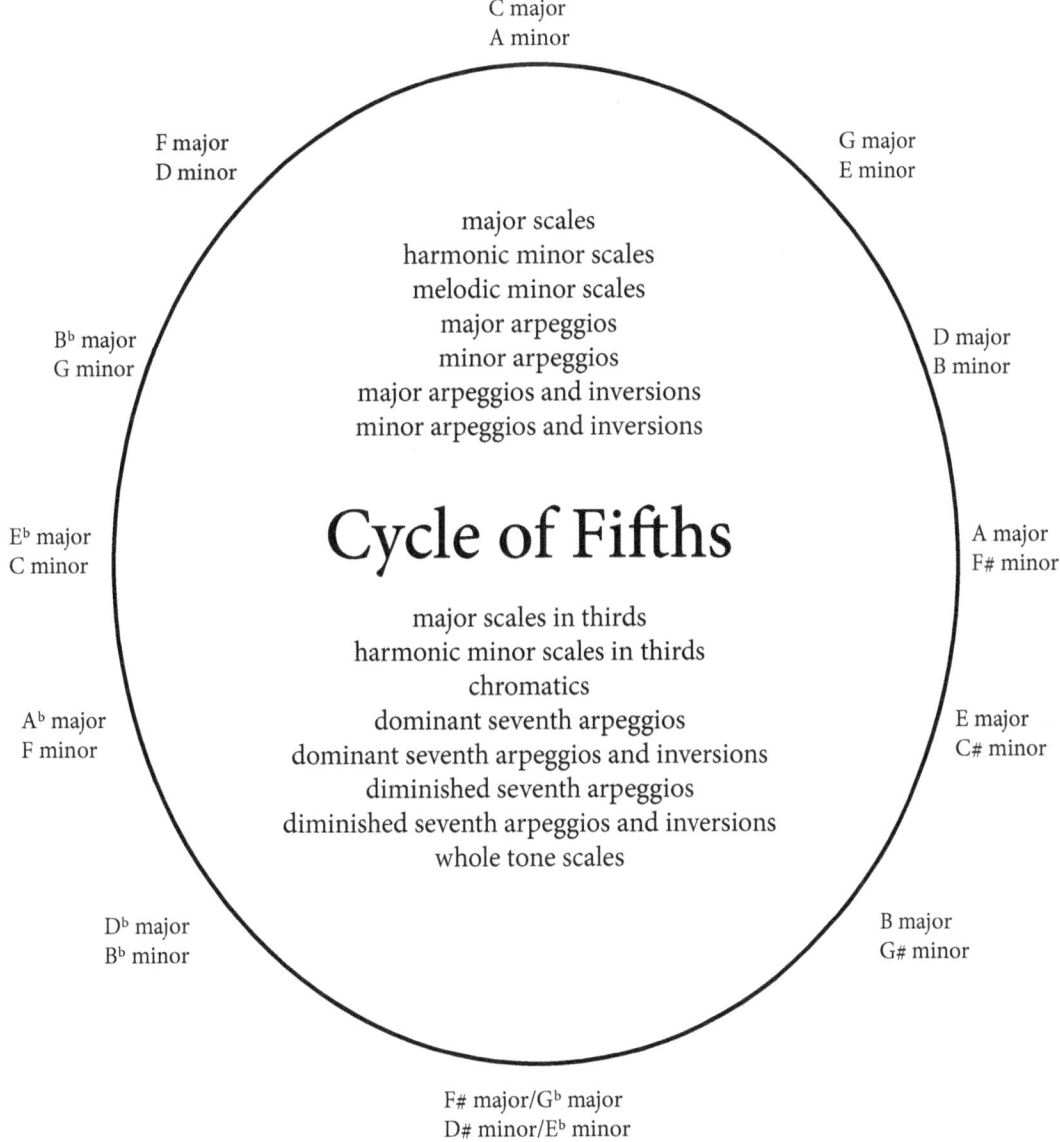

SHARPS ⟶ F C G D A E B ⟵ FLATS

©Peter Bartels 2017
peterbartelsflute.com

Brushing your teeth

No doubt that everyday you brush your teeth. You don't question it, you just do it because you know it's good for you. With the same mind set, I think you should play all your major, harmonic minor and melodic minor scales every single day. It doesn't take very long so don't question it, just do it. You could also add on major and minor broken chords to complete the set. This is in addition to your Key Of The Week work, not instead of it! Play them with the range that suits your level of ability with an eye to extending your horizons. For example if you are playing one octave scales then start extending them out to two octaves and then your two octave scales over the entire range. Challenge yourself and go all the way up to top *C#* or *D*. You should do this with a metronome and keep track of your tempo, using a variety of articulation patterns as well. Have you brushed your teeth today?

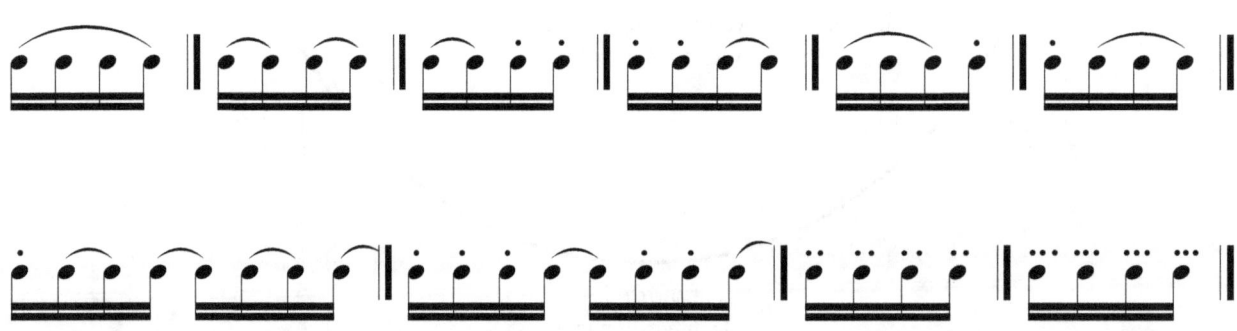

Key of the week

One approach that I found tremendously useful in developing my technique is Key Of The Week. The idea is that you choose one key and stick to it for the whole week using the following series of exercises, that have already appeared in the scales chapter of this book. Aim for curved relaxed fingers and keep the movement to a minimum. Use a metronome and you'll notice that over time you can increase the tempo significantly. It is important to keep track of which keys you have completed so choose a day in the week that will be your key change day, perhaps your lesson day, and write it down somewhere. Over 24 weeks you can cover all major and minor keys. Then go back and do it all again! You can choose any order of keys you like but perhaps begin with familiar keys or even the tonic keys of the repertoire you are playing at the moment.

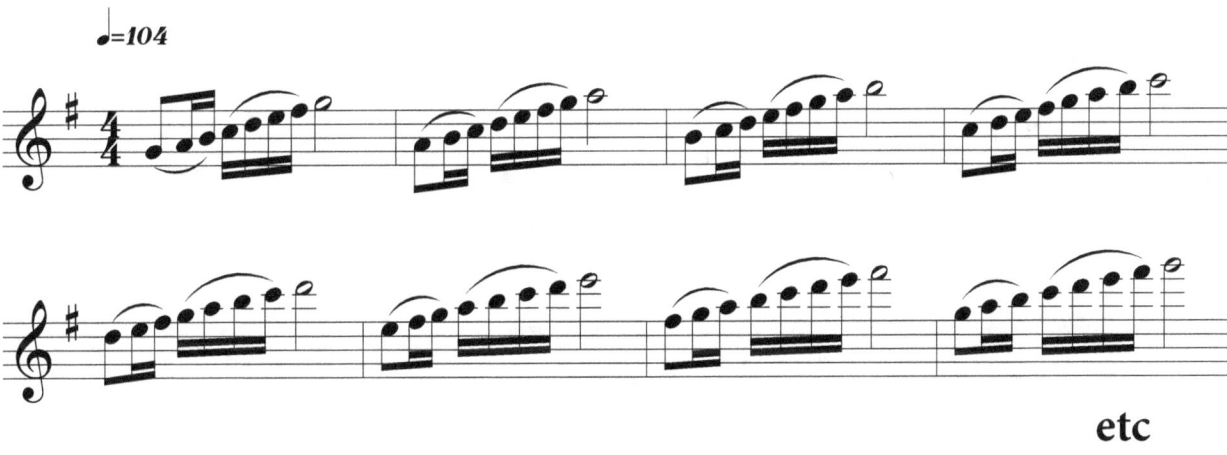

110 Supercharge Your Flute Technique

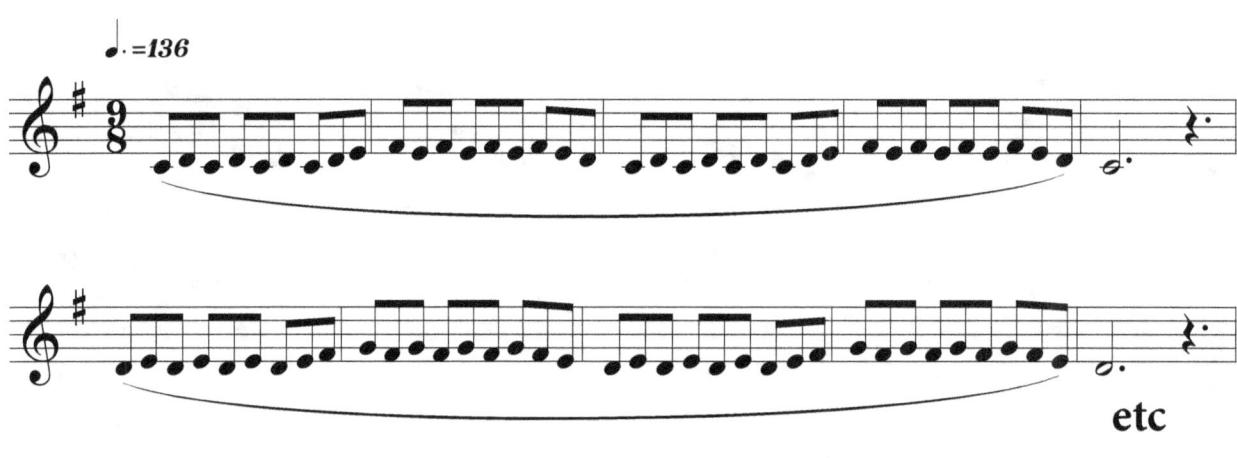

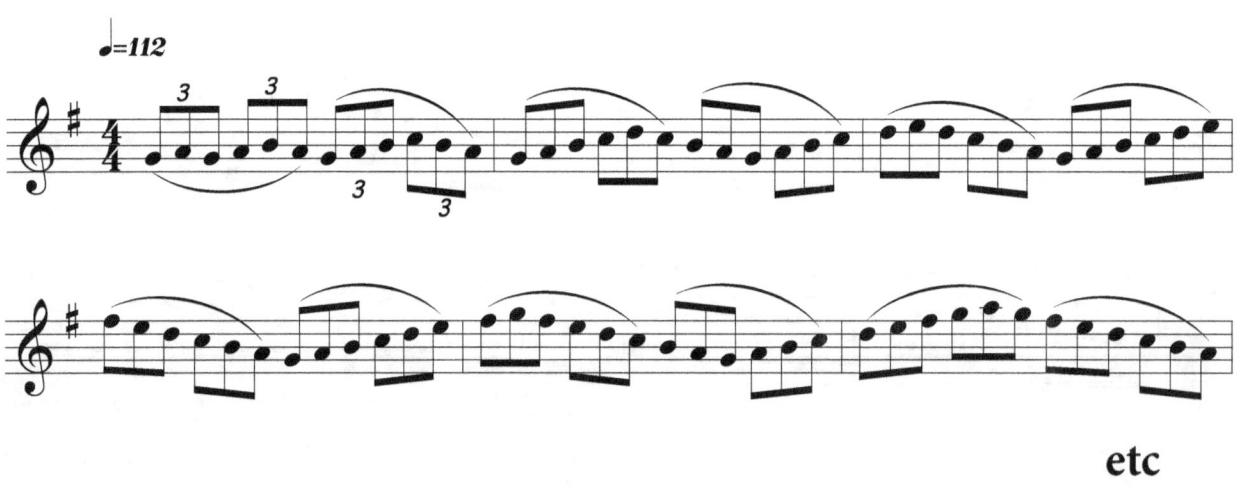

©Peter Bartels 2017
peterbartelsflute.com

Charts

As simple as it seems, I find keeping a written track of my practice very useful. I am a fan of creating my own charts to keep a record of what I am doing. This stops me from practicing only the exercises I like and avoiding the ones that I don't like. Below is an example of a chart I created using a few exercises from chapters in this book. In the corresponding box simply tick when you've completed that exercise in that key or be more specific and note down your tempo and/or articulation patterns as well. A chart like this keeps you honest so go ahead and create your own chart using your own selection of exercises from this book.

	Modal Scales	Loopy Scale Challenge	Intensive Five Note Scale Blitz	Fibonacci Scale	Continuously Expanding Arpeggios	Semiquaver Broken Chords	Chromatic Pillar Notes	Thirds Looping Around
C major/minors								
C#/Db major/minors								
D major/minors								
Eb/D# major/minors								
Eb/D# minors								
E major/minors								
F major/minors								
F#/Gb major/minors								
G major/minors								
Ab/G# major/minors								
A major/minors								
Bb major/minors								
B major/minors								

©Peter Bartels 2017
peterbartelsflute.com

Everything from a single pitch

Another approach to organising your practice that I like is to play everything from the same, single, central pitch. So rather than choosing an exercise and playing it in lots of different keys, you swap the idea around and choose a pitch and play lots of exercises from that central pitch. This book is an example of this idea as the majority of the exercises are given in G major. Some fine flautists do this on as many technical elements as they can such as their scales, arpeggios, chromatics, so adapt this idea using exercises from this book instead. It is not that dissimilar from the chart idea on the previous page except this way around the pitch is central and constant while the exercises float around it, rather than doing one exercise in all the different keys. You could change your central pitch each day or organise it anyway you prefer. Of course a chart would be a great way to keep track of it!

Play the seven exercises from one pitch before moving on.

	C	C#/Db	D	Eb/D#	E	F	F#/Gb	G	G#/Ab	A	Bb/A#	B
Scale Challenge												
Block Scales												
9/8 Fine Finger Movement												
Whole Tone Scales												
Arpeggios in 3/8												
Chromatics pausing at the octaves												
Thirds in manageable blocks												

©Peter Bartels 2017
peterbartelsflute.com